Nayef R.F. A

The Five Dimensions of ...

The Five Dimensions of Global Security

Proposal for a
Multi-sum Security Principle

Nayef R.F. Al-Rodhan

LIT

Gedruckt auf alterungsbeständigem Werkdruckpapier entsprechend
ANSI Z3948   DIN ISO 9706

Bibliographic information published by the Deutsche Nationalbibliothek
The Deutsche Nationalbibliothek lists this publication in the Deutsche
Nationalbibliografie; detailed bibliographic data are available in the Internet at
http://dnb.d-nb.de.

ISBN 978-3-03735-164-0 (Switzerland)
ISBN 978-3-8258-0478-7 (Germany)

© LIT VERLAG GmbH & Co. KG Wien,   LIT VERLAG Dr. W. Hopf
Zweigniederlassung Zürich 2007   Berlin
Dufourstr. 31   Chausseestr. 128–29
CH-8008 Zürich   D-10115 Berlin
Tel. +41 (0) 44-251 75 05
Fax +41 (0) 44-251 75 06
e-Mail: zuerich@lit-verlag.ch
http://www.lit-verlag.ch

Auslieferung:
Deutschland: LIT Verlag Fresnostr. 2, D-48159 Münster
Tel. +49 (0) 2 51/620 32 - 22, Fax +49 (0) 2 51/922 60 99, e-Mail: vertrieb@lit-verlag.de

Distributed in the UK by: Global Book Marketing, 99B Wallis Rd, London, E9 5LN
Phone: +44 (0) 20 8533 5800 – Fax: +44 (0) 1600 775 663
http://www.centralbooks.co.uk/acatalog/search.html

Distributed in North America by:

Transaction Publishers
New Brunswick (U.S.A.) and London (U.K.)

Transaction Publishers
Rutgers University
35 Berrue Circle
Piscataway, NJ 08854

Phone: +1 (732) 445 - 2280
Fax: + 1 (732) 445 - 3138
for orders (U. S. only):
toll free (888) 999 - 6778
e-mail:
orders@transactionspub.com

Contents

	Acknowledgements	7
1	**Introduction**	9
	1. New Approaches to Security	10
	2. A Proposal for a New Security Principle	15
	3. Overview of the Book	16
2	**A Proposed New Classification of Global Security**	19
	1. Introduction	19
	2. The Realist Security Paradigm: The Security Dilemma	20
	3. Collective Security: Mitigating the Security Dilemma	23
	4. Widening the Security Agenda: The Sectoral Approach	24
	5. Deepening the Security Agenda: The Human-Security Paradigm	26
	6. Deepening and Widening the Agenda: Cooperative Security	27
	7. A New Classification of Global Security: The Five Dimensions of Global Security	28
	8. A New Security Principle: The Multi-sum Security Principle	31
	9. Conclusion	33
3	**The Five Dimensions of Global Security**	35
	1. Introduction	35
	2. Human Security	36
	3. Environmental Security	47
	4. National Security	59
	5. Transnational Security	72
	6. Transcultural Security	78
	7. Conclusion	84

4	**Justice as a Prerequisite for Security**	**87**
	1. Introduction	87
	2. Injustice and Insecurity	88
	3. Justice and Long-term Security	94
	4. Conclusion	96
5	**The Multi-sum Security Principle**	**99**
	1. Introduction	99
	2. The Multi-sum Security Principle	100
	3. Multi-sum Security in Practice	106
	4. Conclusion	114
6	**Good Governance**	**117**
	1. Introduction	117
	2. Good Domestic Governance	118
	3. Good Regional Governance	121
	4. Good Global Governance	122
	5. Conclusion	127
7	**Conclusion**	**129**
	References	139
	Index	149

Acknowledgements

This book was written in collaboration with **Lisa Watanabe** from the Program on the Geopolitical Implications of Globalization and Transnational Security at the Geneva Centre for Security Policy.

Dr. Pál Dunay (Hungarian Institute of International Affairs) deserves special thanks for his very constructive and valuable comments on the manuscript.

I am also grateful to Bethany Webster for her invaluable role in coordinating the production of this manuscript.

Ekaterina Rykovanova, Lyubov Nazaruk, Flore-Anne Bourgeois, and Sara Kuepfer also merit thanks for their work.

Lastly, the author would like to express appreciation to Dr. Fred Tanner and the faculty and staff of the Geneva Centre for Security Policy for their unfaltering support.

The views expressed in this book are entirely those of the author and do not necessarily reflect those of the Geneva Centre for Security Policy (GCSP).

CHAPTER 1

INTRODUCTION

In 2002, there were approximately 30 conflicts worldwide.[1]

In 2003, there were 19 major armed conflicts.[2]

In 2003, there were 27,314 reported deaths as a result of political violence.[3]

According to a recently published, but contested, Lancet *survey, there have been 654,965 excess war-related deaths since the 2003 invasion of Iraq.*[4]

In 2004, global defense expenditures totaled more than $1 trillion.[5]

The cost of the war in Iraq has reached some $320 billion.[6]

Some 300,000 child soldiers are involved in more than 30 conflicts worldwide.[7]

In 2004, there were at least 11 international tribunals and countries prosecuting grave human-rights abuses.[8]

Nearly one-fifth, 19.4 percent, of the population of the developing world was living on less than $1 per day in 2002.[9]

If we are to have any hope of improving these numbers, we need to devise ways of addressing the root causes of the multitude of security challenges facing us. This book contributes to this aim by setting out a new security principle. Its inception owes much to the numerous contributions of those academics and practitioners who have called into question the primacy of the state and the military in both academic and practical approaches to security. The search for more adequate approaches to security has taken a number of turns over the last decade and a half. Some have emphasized the possibility of overcoming the negative implications of international anarchy through collective security, thus not fully abandoning the traditional focus on the state and the military. Others have distanced themselves further from the traditional security paradigm by widening the scope of security to include sectors other than the military. In addition, the emergence of a human-security paradigm has called into question the habitual focus on the state as the object that is to be secured to an even greater extent, arguing that the individual, and not the state, should be the primary focus of security. Others still have combined dimensions of all of the above.

Today, it seems fair to say that it is widely recognized that security involves more than the accumulation of military power. Most policy makers and academics would not argue with the claim that security may be enhanced through, for example, increased police cooperation, institution-building within new states, and the democratic reform of armed forces. Moreover, many would go a step further and claim that human security should be at the center of our attention and of policy agendas. These advancements notwithstanding, we propose an even more comprehensive approach to security. This requires outlining a more complete classification of global security that allows for the consideration of a number of referent objects of security. It also means developing a framework for the pursuit of security that focuses on issues other than those linked to the use of military force.

The next section contains a discussion of the new approaches to security that have served to change the field of Security Studies, as well as an assessment of their contributions to the reconceptualization of security. The subsequent section sets out the argument made in the book and briefly outlines the chapters.

1. New Approaches to Security

The discipline of International Relations (IR) has traditionally been governed by realist thinking. In the field of Security Studies, the realist security paradigm – the old state-centered and militaristic view of security – has reigned supreme for many years. According to the realist approach, states are the primary source of both security and insecurity. According to the proponents of this view, states will inevitably suffer from insecurity as long as there is no overarching authority structure in the international system. In the absence of a higher political authority that can guarantee security, states, which are assumed to be rational entities, will make similar strategic calculations. Each will seek to acquire military power in order to deter an attack. Since no supranational authority exists, states have only themselves to rely on for security, making the international security system a self-help system characterized by the security dilemma.[10]

The "logic" of the security dilemma has been contested by those informed by liberal or idealistic principles, who contend that the negative implications of international anarchy can be modified through the creation of rules and norms that govern state behavior, such as that informing the practice of *collective security*, for example. Yet, despite the tremendous contribution of the United Nations (UN) to global security and stability, the concept of collective security does not depart significantly from the traditional security paradigm's military- and state-centrism. As the Cold War came to an end, the preoccupation with interstate conflict gave way to a number of other security issues, such as intrastate conflict. A number of other issues were also recognized as security concerns, including illegal immigration, environmental degradation, organized criminality, and terrorism. As a result, a greater departure from the traditional approach to security was thought to be required.

Accordingly, a debate ensued between those seeking to broaden the scope of Security Studies and those who sought to preserve a narrower focus.[11] Those in favor of widening the agenda argued that issues traditionally associated with domestic policy, such as health, the environment, immigration, and rights, ought to be viewed as global security issues. Given this altered focus, the means of achieving security necessarily extended beyond the use of force and deterrence. An increasing number of IR scholars, including some neorealists, called for a widening of the security agenda. For example, the Copenhagen School sought to set out a framework for security capable of incorporating a wider security agenda. It aimed to establish a more radical view of Security Studies by including both military and nonmilitary issues and the securitization of those threats (i.e., a way of distinguishing security from merely political issues). Their so-called *sectoral approach* classified security into five principal substrates: military, political, economic, environmental, and societal security.[12]

Efforts to increase the scope of security have been accompanied by attempts to challenge the military- and state-centrism of the traditional security paradigm on a more fundamental level through the *concept of human security*, which refocuses security on the individual rather than the state. By focusing on the individual, the numerous ways that human welfare is affected by different phenomena, such as environmental degradation, poor governance, and organized crime, could more adequately be captured.

Many of the issues rendered more visible by a widening of the security agenda and the concept of human security were transboundary in nature in that they transgress the boundaries of individual states and thus affect a number of states at once. This means that effectively addressing such security challenges requires cooperation between states. In many respects, in response to the realization that states needed to cooperate in order to tackle many of the multifarious security challenges identified during the post-Cold War era, a ***cooperative-security concept*** was elaborated in the late 1990s. According to this concept, national security was no longer just a national concern; rather, it was also transnational in that no state can claim or achieve security through its own efforts alone. In elaborate form, cooperative security combined many dimensions of all of the above efforts to reconceptualize security, but it went beyond each individual contribution. It went further than the concept of collective security in that it emphasized achieving security with other states, as well as against them when necessary.[13] In some versions, it called for cooperation between states not only in efforts to tackle transnational security challenges, but also to promote human security within a zone of cooperative security, as well as beyond it.

Security through cooperation is imperative in a world in which threats to security are often transnational. Transnational security threats are non-military in nature and transcend a number of state borders, threatening the political, social, or economic integrity of a state. The primary agents driving many transnational threats are often non-state actors, such as criminal and terrorist networks, and traffickers of various kinds. This creates considerable problems for states and state-based arrangements that have been established to deal with more traditional, military-security challenges. It also encapsulates the sense in which national borders demarcating separations between national economies and ethical norms are less important than they once were. The focus on individual or human security, for example, implies that universal human-rights norms override the principle of non-interference that had previously been crucial to state sovereignty.

We propose classifying global security into five substrates: human, environmental, national, transnational, and transcultural security. While analytically separate, there is, of course, a great deal of overlap between them. Our motivation for this classification is our concern with the human condition, the biosphere, good governance at the state level, the need for cooperation between states, and the cost of suspicion, frustration, and anger as a result of exclusionary collective identities. The first four substrates are, as indicated, represented in one form or another in the above-mentioned approaches to security. These four referents largely capture the essence of both the sectoral and cooperative approaches. However, one facet of global security that has not yet received sufficient attention is transcultural security. In our view, Security Studies should be concerned not only with threats posed to individuals, the environment, and states, but also with cultural and civilizational interactions. Unfortunately, cultural and civilizational questions have been sorely lacking in security thinking, with the exception of the Copenhagen School's concept of societal security, which suggests that there exist within states collective identities that are not necessarily coterminous with the state that may become securitized (i.e., elevated to a security concern). The identification of the security of groups and cultures within states is particularly important within the context of transnational realities, including migration and irregular immigration and xenophobic and exclusionary tendencies in host societies with regard to culture, political beliefs, and religion. A better understanding of different cultures and greater tolerance and respect for diversity could help to prevent or at least mitigate some of the most pressing security concerns of our day.

At the level of the international political community, alliance-building and the coexistence of civilizations are critical when dealing with transnational threats to security. Nevertheless, the end that we have in mind is not simply coexistence between cultural groups and civilizational forms. We argue that a synergy must be found within these cultural groups and civilizational forms, even if competition and non-violent conflict can sometimes generate improvements in the human condition. This is particularly the case in an age of intensified transcultural interaction. When acting together, individual cultures and civilizations can have a greater impact on global security than any individual culture or civilization could when acting independently. Thus, a plurality of cultures can have a net effect on global security that is greater than would be the case if representatives of individual cultures acted individually. This we might think of as transcultural synergy. Transcultural security is a vital component of enhancing security globally, with the eventual goal of achieving transcultural synergy.

While the means of ensuring that these five aspects of security are achieved are likely to be wide-ranging, we believe that attaining justice should be at the heart of long-term solutions to security issues. The pursuit of justice is, therefore, central to our proposed security principle, **the multi-sum security principle**. In general terms, justice may be defined as the correct distribution of benefits and burdens. What justice may require in the domestic realm has received considerable attention. However, its application to the international sphere is a far more contested subject. Within the context of globalization, debates about global justice have, nevertheless, been underway. Here, justice concerns include the gap between rich and poor, the vulnerability of people to abuse, violence, occupation, exclusion, humiliation, disease, and starvation.

Justice, in our view, is a fundamental security concern. Where injustice is present, feelings of frustration, anger, and humiliation are likely to result. This can lead people to experience alienation from the societies and institutions that are supposed to represent them and extreme forms of behavior. Deploying military force alone in the pursuit of security will not be sufficient or even appropriate in instances where groups, states, or sub-national or supranational non-state cultures feel they are the victims of injustice. People intent on This propagating insecurity and instability will find fertile ground for their arguments in places where injustice continues to form part of people's lives.

Of course, this has immediate relevance in relation to the so-called war on terror. While *international terrorism is completely unacceptable, whatever its causes,* confusion resulting from rapid modernization within a globalizing international system has seemed to increase the appeal of messages being propagated by international terrorist networks. In response to a seemingly unjust and largely economic form of globalization, which appears to be accompanied by the spread of a banal form of cosmopolitanism that amounts to little more than consumerism, people may feel that their cultural specificity is under threat. New technologies and increased ease of travel also mean that that people are increasingly aware of what is occurring elsewhere in the world. In addition to enhancing mutual awareness, this may also result in a heightened awareness of injustices as a result of political oppression, abuse, and discrimination. Terrorist networks also thrive on the failure of states, as well as the international community, to deliver promote some form basic social justice. Seen from this angle, addressing the root causes of international terrorism clearly requires cooperation between states, mostly through non-military means. Military force alone is unlikely to diminish the number of people being recruited daily by international terrorist groups. If we wish to do so, we must recognize the importance of considerations of justice.

The precise form that justice may take is likely to depend on the specifics of particular problems. While it may appear obvious that justice should inform state policies, conflict prevention and conflict resolution, and rebuilding war-torn societies, it is all too often not the case. In order to contribute to global justice, all governments should be committed to international and international humanitarian law without reservations.

Creating the conditions under which lasting security can become a reality will require good governance. At the domestic level, the promotion of justice for individuals, states, and cultures requires a combination of respect for civil liberties, accountability and transparency, protection of the country and population, the pursuit of sustainable growth, tolerance and respect for diversity, and adequate representation of the people. At the regional level, good governance requires the establishment of representative, transparent, and accountable institutions and practices. Good global governance also involves the pursuit of global justice. But the international community as an agency-bearing entity suffers from a number of shortcomings, and possibilities are circumvented by the continued salience of short-sighted conceptions of national interest.

Without justice, security at all levels will prove elusive, because in a globalized world, the security of any state or culture cannot be disconnected from that of others and, therefore, cannot be achieved without ensuring security through *justice* for *all* individuals, states, and cultures, no matter how challenging this may be.

2. A Proposal for a New Security Principle

In an effort to contribute to a more inclusive approach to global security, we wish to propose a new principle of security, which we will call the **multi-sum security principle**, which states that: **"In a globalized world, security can no longer be thought of as a zero-sum game involving states alone. Global security, instead, has five di-**

mensions that include **human, environmental, national, transnational, and transcultural security**, and, therefore, global security and the security of any state or culture cannot be achieved without good governance at all levels that guarantees security through *justice* for *all* individuals, states, and cultures."

This principle aims not only to promote cooperative interaction between states that looks both inwards and outwards, but also a certain degree of cohesiveness that is required both within and between countries in order to enhance stability and security.

The five dimensions of global security include five substrates of modern security: **human, environmental, national, transnational, and transcultural.** The first is human security, which, as mentioned, refers to the security of individuals. The second is environmental security, which refers to the security of the biosphere. The third is national security, referring to the more traditional economic, societal (state population), political, and military dimensions of national security. The fourth, transnational security, involves security against transnational threats that refer to any type of illegal cross-border movements. The fifth, transcultural security, refers to the integrity of large collective identities.

3. Overview of the Book

The first section of Chapter 2 reviews existing approaches to global security in order to elucidate the points of departure of our proposed new security principle. Then, in the second section, we put forward our own classification of global security. Having proposed this new classification of security, which allows for a variation of referent objects, as well as a variety of means with which to enhance security, we briefly introduce our new security principle, the **multi-sum security principle.**

In Chapter 3, we outline our new classification of global security in greater detail. We argue that global security may be thought of analytically as comprising five dimensions of security. In each of the subsequent sections, we discuss each substrate of global security in turn. Within each respective section, we define our understanding of each substrate, highlight some of the major issues of each of the five dimensions of global security, and specify some of the achievements and outstanding challenges within each substrate.

Chapter 4 focuses on the security implications of injustice and the significance of justice for the advancement of global security. We argue that justice must be viewed as a fundamental security concern. Nevertheless, it is all too often ignored by policy makers, or it is viewed as a question of philosophy rather than national security. As we have highlighted, however, many security challenges are at some level spawned by injustice of one sort or another. For this reason, justice constitutes a vital dimension of our multi-sum security principle. We begin by looking at the relationship between injustice and feelings of frustration, anger, and humiliation. We suggest that such sentiments are generated by alienation, which often provokes extreme forms of action. We then briefly examine some contemporary examples of how real or perceived injustice can help to generate a sense of humiliation, alienation, feelings of frustration, and anger. Lastly, we argue that justice is imperative if lasting security and stability are to be achieved. Thus, we suggest that attempting to deal with many security problems by resorting to the use of military force will not be effective as long as real or perceived injustice continues to exist. This, we argue, is because people who feel alienated also feel dispossessed of their agency, and as long as this is the case they will use whatever means available to them to try to regain it and to be faithful to their true evaluative commitments. Moreover, as long as injustices persist, people who wish to propagate insecurity and instability will find an audience for their ideas, no matter how illogical, futile, or violent. Therefore, without justice, long-term security will be forever ephemeral.

Respect for people's equal worth, whether in terms of identity and dignity or their cultural, ethnic, and religious diversity, is vital to promoting greater justice. Efforts to reduce structural economic and political inequalities that contribute to alienation and possible conflict are also vital to the cause of justice. People are driven to extremes because they cannot express their frustrations, their anger, their hopes, and their fears through regular political channels. The attainment of justice allows people to regain their full agency as human beings capable of defining themselves and their lives in a way that is authentic to them. One of the most vital things to understand when promoting greater justice is the significance of empowerment.

In Chapter 5, we provide a detailed explanation of our new security principle, the ***multi-sum security principle***. This principle draws together our proposed classification of global security, which comprises five dimensions of security – human, environmental, national, transnational, and transcultural security – and the notion that justice is a prerequisite for security. Having outlined the principle, we then explore the relationship between injustice and insecurity within the five substrates of global security and suggest what it might mean to pursue justice in each of our substrates.

The last chapter deals with the question of good governance. At the domestic level, we claim that good governance involves the protection of basic civil and human rights, inclusivity (socioeconomic, cultural, and political), and effective institutions (impartial, transparent, and accountable). In our view, however, good global governance entails overlapping structures of authority. While states are still relevant, they do not form the only locus of authority. Where governance structures at the regional level already exist, they should be participatory, transparent, and accountable, taking on transnational questions that cannot be dealt with adequately at the state level. Where they are still lacking, they should be established. At the global level, we claim that good governance implies the primacy of cosmopolitan law, effective multilateralism and multilateral bodies, economic cosmopolitanism, and the promotion of ways of increasing peaceful coexistence and exchanges between civilizations.

CHAPTER 2

A PROPOSED NEW CLASSIFICATION OF GLOBAL SECURITY

1. Introduction

Within the traditional conception of security, expounded by the realist school of IR, the referent object of security is the state. For realists, security essentially means securing the integrity of the state. If the state is secure, it is assumed that its citizens will also be secure. Security is thought to be achieved through accumulation, primarily, of military power and ensuring the credibility of its use.

While the realist security paradigm dominated IR thinking during the Cold War years, the concept of security underwent a process of both broadening and deepening once the Cold War ended. Those in favor of broadening the agenda argued that issues traditionally associated with domestic policy, such as health, the environment, migration, and rights, should be recast as security issues. With this altered focus, the means of achieving security necessarily extended beyond the use of force and deterrence. Many of these issues were also transboundary in nature, signifying that the state could no longer rely on self-help for security.

Others departed even further from the realist security paradigm by arguing that the individual rather than the state should be the central referent object of security. As a result, human security was proposed as a competing security paradigm. Shifting the object of security to the individual meant that security was understood as freedom from fear and want, and the means of achieving it were multifaceted.

In our view, Security Studies should be concerned not only with transnational threats posed to individuals and the state, but also with cultural and civilizational interactions. Unfortunately, cultural and civilizational questions have been neglected in security thinking, with the exception of the Copenhagen School's concept of societal security. Yet, a better understanding of different cultures and greater tolerance and respect for diversity could help to prevent or at least mitigate some of the most pressing security concerns of our day.

We therefore suggest that global security should be understood as comprising five substrates: human, environmental, national, transnational, and transcultural security. While the means of satisfying these five dimensions of security are likely to be wide-ranging, we contend that the attainment of justice must be central to any long-term solution to security issues. Thus, a fundamental means of achieving security is justice.

With these two thoughts in mind, we put forward a new, alternative security principle, which we hope will contribute to long-term global security. The principle that we are proposing is termed the *multi-sum security principle*, which states that: **"In a globalized world, security can no longer be thought of as a zero-sum game involving states alone. Global security, instead, has five dimensions that include human, environmental, national, transnational, and transcultural security, and, therefore, global security and the security of any state or culture cannot be achieved without good governance at all levels that guarantees security through** *justice* **for** *all* **individuals, states, and cultures."**

2. The Realist Security Paradigm: The Security Dilemma

Within the realist security paradigm, the state constitutes the referent object of security. In other words, in response to the question "What is to be secured?" realists typically answer, "the state." This reflects realism's preoccupation with the state. Within the realist security paradigm, the state is inextricably linked to the use of force. Internally, sovereignty implies a monopoly on the use of force and the capacity to enforce laws. Externally, the sovereign state coexists with other sovereign states in the absence of a higher political authority to enforce order. Thus, in addition to organizing power domestically, one of the main concerns of the state is to accumulate power internationally. Power is typically defined in terms of a combination of economic, technological, diplomatic, and military means.[14] All strands of realism have in common the premise that states strive for power in order to secure their survival.[15]

Why do states struggle for power? Classical realists emphasize what they see as the fundamental characteristics of human nature.

The fundamental cause of conflicts is thus attributed to the drive for power and the selfishness of individuals. Given that human nature is assumed to be unchanging, international conflict is thought to be inevitable. Hans Morgenthau, for example, maintains that international politics characterized as an endless struggle for power is the product of human nature.[16] Since egoism is understood to be an essential facet of human nature, conflict is assumed to be inevitable.

In response to this question, structural or neo-realists emphasize the structure of the international system. For John Herz, for example, it is not human nature but the condition of international anarchy that generates fear, suspicion, and insecurity.[17] A competitive logic is thought to motivate states to accrue power. This logic was given expression in the concept of the *security dilemma*, which was first coined by Herz in 1950. The idea behind the security dilemma is that, in order for a state to be secure, another state is necessarily made insecure. Herz argued that, wherever anarchic societal arrangements have existed, a security dilemma between either individuals, groups, or their leaders had typically emerged. As individuals, groups, or leaders strive to attain security, they are driven to accumulate (mostly) military power. This renders other states less secure, thus causing them to engage in the same drive for power. Herz applied the concept of the security dilemma to the international system, arguing that the same thing is guaranteed to occur among states, since no higher authority exists to enforce order among them.[18]

Kenneth Waltz's later, seminal work *The Theory of International Politics* (1979) further consolidated the notion that insecurity ultimately has structural causes. In contrast to classical realists, Waltz maintained that the uniqueness of international politics lay not in the regularity of war and conflict, since this was also characteristic of domestic politics. Waltz asserted that the key difference between international and domestic politics was in their structure. In the domestic polity, citizens are not obliged to defend themselves. In the international system, there is no higher authority to prevent and counter the use of force. Therefore, security can only be achieved through self-help. In providing for their own security, however, states will automatically make other states insecure.[19]

A number of other consequences flow from the competitive logic of power politics. First, states are assumed to be both the principal source of security *and* insecurity in the realist security paradigm. In the absence of a world government, they are the principal political units that take on the task of providing state security. As independent and armed entities, they are also capable of adversely affecting the security of other states. Effective statecraft, therefore, is thought to involve not only building up and deploying military force, but also ensuring the credibility of its use in order to deter attacks.[20] Within the realist vision of world politics, achieving security is a zero-sum game.

Second, security competition prevents states from agreeing on universal principles, with the exception of the principle of non-intervention.[21] The skeptical interpretation of human nature and the motivation of states also means that moral considerations in international relations are thought to be subordinate to the imperative of survival and the resulting pursuit of power.[22] This is not to say that all realists exclude the possibility of moral considerations in state policy. Some classical realists, such as Morgenthau, argue that human beings are motivated not only by the pursuit of power, but also by the pursuit of justice. E.H. Carr argued that "we cannot ultimately find a resting place in pure realism."[23] Nevertheless, in the final analysis, greater weight is given either to egoistic passions or the constraints of international anarchy.

Realists diverge on the question of whether states can escape the constraints imposed on them by the security dilemma. Classical realists argue that the security dilemma can be minimized through the balance of power. They claim that, throughout the history of the state system, balances of power have emerged. Structural realists believe that power balances are an enduring characteristic of the international system and that maintaining a balance of power became a central objective in the foreign policies of the Great Powers. All agree, however, that balances of power are unstable. Moreover, egoism, whether the result of human nature or the anarchical structure of the international system, militates against the provision of collective goods, such as collective security.[24] Alliances and cooperative arrangements between states are unlikely to last.

In sum, in the realist security paradigm, the state is the main referent object of security, security competition exists as a result of the condition of international anarchy, and the result is that the international state system is a self-help system in which the pursuit of security is a zero-sum struggle for power, largely defined in military terms.

3. Collective Security: Mitigating the Security Dilemma

Since the struggle for power and self-help are given priority in the realist security paradigm, institutions are not believed to have a significant role to play in enhancing security and preventing war. Institutions are viewed as the product of state interest and the constraints imposed upon them by international anarchy. In contrast to this view, other approaches to international security exist that take power politics seriously, but that also leave room for domestic politics, norms, and beliefs to inform international politics.

Proponents of *collective security* argue that, while military force remains an important characteristic of international life, there are realistic opportunities to mitigate the security dilemma and to move beyond self-help in international politics. For many authors of the so-called English School of IR, such as Martin Wight, the formal anarchical structure of the international system need not necessarily lead to the presence of the security dilemma, since the international state system has evolved rules and practices that channel state-to-state relations and enable a certain degree of order to develop.[25]

Collective security essentially requires states to renounce the use of force to alter the status quo and to settle all of their disputes in a peaceful manner. It also implies that states broaden their conception of national interest to incorporate the overall interests of the international community. This means that, when an aggressor appears in the system, all of the responsible states in the collective-security zone confront the aggressor with overwhelming military power. By facing aggressors together, collective security is seen as providing deterrence and more effective action in the event that deterrence fails. In addition, collective-security institutions are also thought to facilitate greater confidence within the international system. Thus the aim of collective security is to dampen security competition between states.[26]

At the practical level, liberal or idealistic thinking has informed various attempts to promote collective security. The concept of collective security refers to the collective effort of a plurality of states to ensure security among one other. The League of Nations constituted a prominent example of the concept of collective security in practice. The League was perceived as a government of governments, settling disputes between individual states in an open and legalistic manner. Its members vowed to protect each other from attack by other states, through the use of force if required. Following the end of World War II, the UN took on this function at the global level.[27]

Despite the tremendous contribution of the UN and other collective-security fora, such as the North Atlantic Treaty Organisation (NATO), the concept of collective security is now deemed to be too narrow to meet contemporary security challenges. Interstate conflict is arguably giving way to increased intrastate conflict, partly as a result of the artificial boundaries imposed by colonial powers on many countries in Africa and the rest of the developing world, as well as the collapse of the Soviet Union. Minority or ethnic communities are also expanding as a result of increased migration and refugee flows. Ethnic and religious differences are sometimes used for political ends, often leading to conflict.[28] Moreover, a number of other issues, such as the environment, organized criminality, and terrorism, have also come to be seen as security concerns. Important as "high" politics, involving military (and sometimes economic) issues in interstate conflict might be, "low" politics are also important security concerns. This implies that the state should not always be given priority as the referent object of security.

4. Widening the Security Agenda: The Sectoral Approach

In response to these concerns, an increasing number of IR scholars, including some neo-realists, have called for a widening of the security agenda in recent years. Some scholars feared that, with the broadening of the security agenda to include an ever greater array of issues, such as the environment, welfare, and immigration, that more areas of life would become "securitized." The objection that some scholars had was that the fundamental meaning of security remained unchanged. Invoking these issues as security concerns still implied the notion of threat and defense, and continued to give the state a primary role in the provision of security. Security as a concept is, thus, simply borrowed from the traditional security paradigm and applied to a wider range of areas. The concept of security still referred to the state.

In 1983, for example, Barry Buzan attempted to show how expanding the security agenda might be handled otherwise by identifying economic, military, societal, and environmental "sectors" of security.[29] National security, however, remained privileged. In his 1991 version, he clarifies that national security is prioritized, but that it cannot be understood with reference to the state alone. What he succeeded in demonstrating was that national security could neither be comprehended nor achieved by the state alone.

Ole Waever argued that the danger with widening the security agenda without redefining the concept entailed the risk that elites would securitize issues in order to gain control of the state. In his conception, something is a security issue when state elites identify it as such. Security, he argued, may be understood as a speech act. Security implies a situation characterized by an identified security problem and some measure taken in response to it. Insecurity is viewed as a situation marked by a security problem with no response to it. In Waever's view, removing a security problem cannot happen by treating it in security terms, only by "desecuritizing" it, for instance by dealing with it as a political issue.[30]

The Copenhagen School's attempt to develop a new comprehensive framework for Security Studies grew out of these attempts to question the centrality of military-security issues in interstate conflict and to suggest other possible referent objects of security.

Barry Buzan, Ole Waever, and Jaap de Wilde were among the prominent figures that sought to set out a framework capable of incorporating the wider agenda developing within both policy and academic circles. They aimed to establish a more radical view of Security Studies by exploring threats to referent objects (state and non-state), and the securitization of those threats (i.e., a way of distinguishing security from merely political issues).

They proposed a so-called ***sectoral approach*** that identified five principal sectors of security: military, political, economic, environmental, and societal. In the military sector, the referent object of security is typically the state, though it may also be other types of political entities. The realist security paradigm tends to view all military affairs as security issues. However, as Buzan, Waever, and de Wilde point out, this may not always be the case. For many states, defense of the state is simply one function of the military today. Their militaries are likely to be increasingly called upon to engage in peace-support missions. In the political sector, political threats are usually defined in terms of threats to sovereignty, but sometimes also to the ideology of the state. The economic sector, which is infrequently identified as a security concern, except when the survival of a population is threatened, may also be invoked as a security issue. In the societal sector, as they define it, the referent objects are large-scale collective identities that function independently from the state, such as nations and religions.[31]

Buzan, Waever, and de Wilde justified their inclusion of objects other than the state by arguing that issues or objects that are raised to the level of security concerns may be considered legitimate referents of security. In their approach, the meaning of the concept of security is therefore linked to its usage rather than something that can be defined analytically. While separated analytically, different sectors were thought to be integrated in the way in which entities integrated them in their policy-making processes at various levels.[32]

Despite its contribution to the transformation of Security Studies, the Copenhagen School did not fully break with the state-centrism of the realist security paradigm. While the sectoral approach allowed for something other than the state to be a referent object of security, only the state can act on issues designated security concerns. Thus, the departure from state-centrism is not complete.[33]

5. Deepening the Security Agenda: The Human-Security Paradigm

Other scholars and practitioners have sought not only to widen the agenda, but also to deepen it through the concept of human security, which constitutes an emerging paradigm of global security. Its proponents believe that a more comprehensive notion of security that draws upon the traditionally separate fields of Development Studies and Security Studies is needed.

Human security challenges the traditional notion of national security by arguing that the proper referent object of security should be the individual rather than the state. A people-centered view of security is thus deemed necessary in order to achieve national, regional, and global security.

The concept was defined and has been employed primarily within the context of the UN system. The United Nations Development Programme's (UNDP) 1994 Human Development Report, *New Dimensions of Human Security*, is considered a milestone publication in the field of human security. It argued that human security consists of two main components: freedom from want and freedom from fear. Within this paradigm, security implies the absence of hunger and illness, respect for human rights and dignity, as well as the absence of violence and armed conflict, which usually inflict considerable suffering on civilians. Threats to human security may be further classified into economic, food, health, environmental, personal, community, and political security.[34]

That said, no single, agreed-upon concept of human security exists. Nevertheless, it is characteristically identified as a global problem that requires a global response, which includes civil-society initiatives.[35] While the inclusiveness of the concept of human security has invited the criticism that it exposes the field to too many concerns, thereby watering it down, we believe that it remains attractive because it captures the assorted factors that contribute to individual insecurity.

6. Deepening and Widening the Agenda: Cooperative Security

The *cooperative-security concept* incorporates dimensions of all of these approaches. Cooperative security implies more than collective security. It involves achieving security *with* others rather than against them.[36] The cooperative-security concept also extends the means of achieving security beyond the use of force and deterrence. Cooperative security goes beyond collective security in that it not only looks inward, ensuring security and stability within a cooperative-security zone, but also outward. Looking outward implies promoting stability outside the cooperative-security space, in the near abroad or even further afield. Indeed, trouble spots in far-flung areas of the globe have become serious security concerns in an age of intensified transnational challenges to security. Mass violations of human rights in Kosovo in 1998 and 1999 caused consternation around the world.[37] Since the end of the Cold War, NATO and the European Union (EU) have actively promoted stability and security in Eastern and Southeastern Europe, primarily through the expansion of their membership. The EU, in particular, demonstrates the promotion of stability by employing "soft" means. The expansion of its membership involves the diffusion of norms that significantly alter the candidate states. It also attempts to enhance stability in the neighboring Mediterranean and Middle East regions through economic cooperation and political dialogue.

In an elaborate formulation of cooperative security, Richard Cohen argues that cooperative security must also include human security. Indeed, from this perspective, the security of the individual is the foundation upon which all other security depends. In a world of growing interconnectivity, the human condition has become a common and basic concern. If the security of people in another state is compromised by outside forces or more often than not by internal forces, many other people now recognize such occurrences as diminishing their own security according to this concept. As a result, the Westphalian concept of a state's right to non-interference is no longer as tenable as it once was. This means that, in contrast to the realist security paradigm, proponents of cooperative security assume that states can and should agree on ethical principles.

Like collective security, the cooperative-security concept calls into question the realist paradigm's assumption that the state system is a self-help system. It assumes that states can engage in lasting cooperation and, moreover, that their security depends upon this. Security, therefore, does not have to be a zero-sum game. This is important, since security through cooperation is imperative in a world in which threats to security are often transnational in nature. While sharing the same conviction that states can engage in cooperative relations and, in so doing, significantly improve their security, it goes beyond the collective-security concept in that it views cooperation as taking a variety of forms in response to a wide array of security challenges, many of which are non-military in nature and require non-military responses. Moreover, the primary actors driving many transnational threats are often non-state actors, such as criminal and terrorist networks, and traffickers of various kinds rather than states. This creates considerable problems for states and state-based arrangements that have been established to deal with more traditional, military-security challenges and reinforces the need to recognize that national security is no longer simply national, but transnational in its dimensions.

7. A New Classification of Global Security: The Five Dimensions of Global Security

In order to take a more inclusive view and approach to global security, we propose a new classification of global security, which includes five dimensions of security: **human, environmental, national, transnational, and transcultural.** These five substrates are presented in figure one in the form of a pentagon.

Figure 1: The Five Dimensions of Global Security

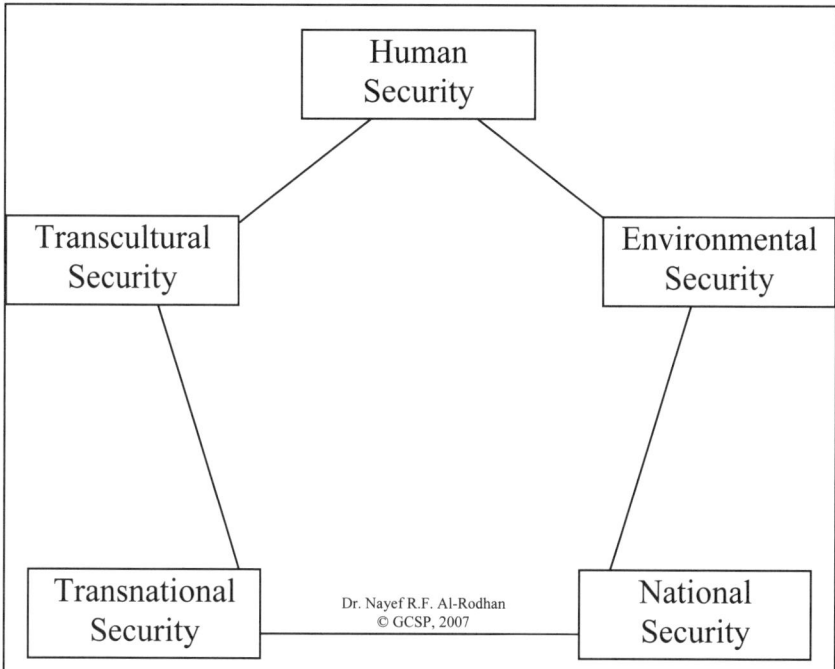

The first substrate is human security, which, as mentioned, refers to the security of individuals. The second is environmental security, which refers to the security of the biosphere. The third is national security, referring to a state's population, economic situation, and organizational integrity. The fourth, transnational security, involves security against transnational threats that refer to any type of illegal transborder phenomenon.

These four referents are largely represented by the sectoral and cooperative-security approaches and the human-security paradigm. Yet, the implications of transnational security challenges are multifaceted and far-reaching, and responses to them must be similar in scope, applicability, and complexity. One element of global security that is missing in the traditional security paradigm is the transcultural element. Therefore, we propose a fifth substrate of security, transcultural security, which refers to ensuring that a plurality of cultures and civilizations can coexist without elevating their relations to security issues. Our classification, therefore, goes beyond the realist security paradigm in an additional sense: It brings culture onto center stage, whereas realism has traditionally marginalized it.

The sectoral approach addressed cultural issues to some extent. Indeed, societal security was perhaps the biggest contribution the approach made to Security Studies. The identification of security of groups and cultures within states is particularly important within the context of transnational realities, including intensified migration and exclusionary tendencies in host societies with regard to culture, political beliefs, and religion. Societal security implied that there are large-scale collective identities that may not be consonant with the state. In the societal approach, large-scale collective identities can exist independently from the state and will vary in time and space.[38]

Whether societal security becomes an issue will, according to Buzan, Waever, and de Wilde, depend on how collective identities respond to external or internal developments. This, in turn, is likely to be contingent on whether the holders of a collective identity take a closed-minded or open-minded view of how their identity is constituted and maintained. Collective identities may be perceived as under threat in relation to issues such as migration or regional integration, for example.[39]

With our fifth substrate of global security, transcultural security, we identify cultures and civilizations as referent objects. We define culture as an advanced awareness of the religious tradition, customs, institutions, or aesthetic accomplishments of a nation or a group. It relates to the individual and group. Civilizational forms are structured by cultures and represent advanced systems of social organization.[40] As is mentioned above, we view cultural issues as important factors influencing the dynamics of the global system. While *culture* and *civilization* are frequently employed interchangeably, it is worth differentiating between them.

In our view, a balance needs to be found between cultural and broader civilizational variations. At the level of the international political community, alliance-building and the coexistence of civilizations are vital when dealing with transnational threats to security. This is especially so in an era of unprecedented transcultural interaction. Yet, we wish to go further by arguing that, when acting together, individual cultures can have a greater impact on global security than any individual culture could have were it to act in isolation. Thus, a plurality of cultures can have a net effect on global security that is greater than would be the case if representatives of individual cultures acted individually. This, we might think of as transcultural synergy, which in our view is the end goal of transcultural security.

8. A New Security Principle: The Multi-sum Security Principle

Having suggested a new classification of global security, which includes five dimensions of security, we propose a new security principle: *the multi-sum security principle.* The principle is defined below in figure 2.

Figure 2: The Multi-sum Security Principle

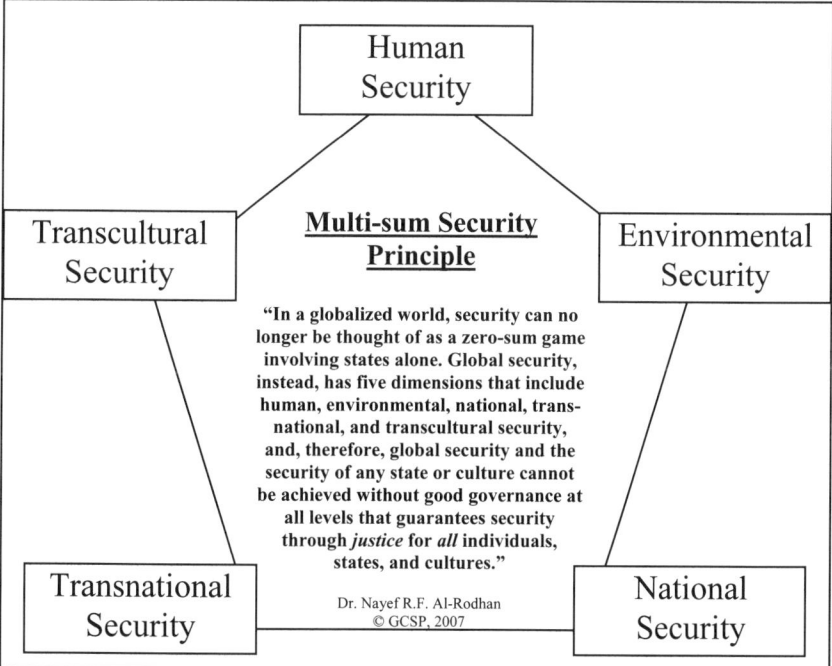

At the core of this principle is the pursuit of justice, which is generally interpreted as the correct allocation of benefits and burdens. Typically, justice has been considered in relation to the domestic realm. Its application to the international sphere has posed greater problems and remains a contentious issue. Global justice is discussed in relation to the gap between rich and poor, the vulnerability of people to abuse, violence, occupation, exclusion, humiliation, disease, and starvation, among other things. Justice is, however, a complex concept. It can refer to treating people equally, righting wrongs done to others, what people may rightfully claim from others, or what people are due, for example.

We submit that justice constitutes a fundamental security concern. For this reason, it forms a central component of our multi-sum security principle. Injustice seems particularly important from a security point of view because of its potential to generate feelings of frustration, anger, and humiliation, which, in turn, are likely to cause people to feel alienated from the societies to which they belong, as well as the institutions that are supposed to serve them. Once the importance of justice to security is acknowledged, it becomes clear that military force will be an inadequate instrument in the pursuit of security if injustices are left to fester. Those who are intent on propagating insecurity and instability will find fertile ground for their ideas as long as real or perceived injustices are left unaddressed. The marginalization of extremism, for example, will prove more challenging as long as a sense of injustice is widespread and deeply felt. While extreme elements in societies will always be a part of life, their appeal will be minimized if justice is systematically pursued. Without justice, long-term and lasting security will be unattainable.

The kind of justice that is entailed is likely to depend on the specifics of the issues at hand. While it may appear obvious that justice is a vital means of achieving security, it is all too often neglected in the formulation of policies, in negotiations to being conflicts to a close, and in situations of post-conflict reconstruction, thus breeding animosity among states and within communities.

Multi-sum security will also depend on good governance. At the domestic level, good governance implies justice for individuals, nations, and cultures is likely to be realized through a combination of respect for civil liberties, accountability and transparency, protection of the country and population, the pursuit of sustainable growth, tolerance and respect for diversity, and adequate representation of the people. Global governance should also facilitate the pursuit of justice. While the international community as an agency-bearing entity suffers from a number of shortcomings, largely due to defined national interests, international law and humanitarian law do, nevertheless, contribute to greater global justice. All governments should, therefore, be unconditionally committed to them. Justice as fairness should also form a central consideration in negotiation processes, as well as be applied throughout the implementation phase of international resolutions. The pursuit of greater justice should also be recognized as critical to a state's ability to secure its population from security threats, not least those stemming from international terrorism. Our multi-sum security principle is in the long-term interests of states and members of diverse cultural groups and civilizations. Indeed, it is our belief that without justice, security at all levels will be frail, because in a globalized world, security can neither be achieved alone nor without seeking *justice* for *all* individuals, states, and cultures, however hard this may be.

9. Conclusion

We began this chapter by reviewing existing approaches to security. We pointed out that the state constituted the main object of security within the realist security paradigm. Moreover, in the absence of a world government, the state system is assumed to be a self-help system in which security is a zero-sum game. The concept of collective security, by contrast, assumes that the negative implications of international anarchy can be mitigated through the creation of norms and rules that channel the behavior of states in a more positive direction. Despite the enormous contribution of practical examples of collective security, the concept was perceived as too limited to adequately capture the nature of the security challenges facing states today. In response to an increased awareness of non-traditional, non-military threats, such as transnational threats, a number of IR scholars, including some realists, set about widening the scope of security to include non-traditional concerns, such as the environment, arms trafficking, and illegal migration. In an attempt to provide a framework for analysis of this expanded focus, the Copenhagen School put forward the sectoral approach, which delineated five sectors of security: military, political, economic, environmental, and societal. Despite the innovative nature and contribution of this approach, it did not quite break with the state-centrism of realism. Where the sectoral approach failed, the human-security paradigm succeeded. It represented a far more radical break with the traditional approach to security, prioritizing the individual over the state. The cooperative-security concept, in its most elaborate formulation, attempted to combine all of these approaches within one framework, arguing that global security depends on the promotion of human security, transnational cooperation, and collective security.

These contributions notwithstanding, we proposed a new classification of global security that allows for the individual and the state to be considered as referent objects of security, but that does not limit referents to these two entities. In addition, we wished to elaborate on the question of culture and to emphasize that the security of diverse cultural groups and civilizational forms is dependent on, at the very least, cooperation between these entities. Therefore, we subdivided global security into five major substrates: human, environmental, national, transnational, and transcultural security. Having proposed this new classification of security, which allows for a variation of referent objects and also a variety of means with which to enhance security, we also put forward a new security principle, which we termed the multi-sum security principle.

CHAPTER 3

THE FIVE DIMENSIONS OF GLOBAL SECURITY

1. Introduction

In the previous chapter, we proposed a new classification of global security, with the aim of providing a more comprehensive vision and approach to global security. We suggested that global security should be thought of analytically as consisting of five dimensions of security. The five dimensions or substrates of global security comprised within the pentagon were identified as human, environmental, national, transnational, and transcultural security.

Having proposed this new classification of security, which allows for a variation of referent objects and also a variety of means with which to enhance security, we also put forward a new security principle, which we termed **the multi-sum security principle,** which states that: **"In a globalized world, security can no longer be thought of as a zero-sum game involving states alone. Global security, instead, has five dimensions that include human, environmental, national, transnational, and transcultural security, and, therefore, global security and the security of any state or culture cannot be achieved without good governance at all levels that guarantees security through** *justice* **for** *all* **individuals, states, and cultures."**

In this chapter, we devote attention to further elaborating our proposed classification of global security. To that end, we discuss each of the substrates of global security – **human, environmental, national, transnational, and transcultural** – individually within each section of the chapter. Within each respective section, we define our understanding of each substrate of global security. We then discuss some of the most prevalent issues within each security domain. Finally, we indicate the achievements and outstanding challenges within each substrate.

2. Human Security

As mentioned in the previous chapter, recent years have seen a movement to deepen, as well as widen, the scope of Security Studies. Those who have sought to deepen the security agenda have attempted to do so by offering a new organizing concept of security, namely human security. Proponents of the human-security paradigm believe that a more comprehensive notion of security is required to adequately address the vulnerabilities faced by individuals by uniting the traditionally discrete fields of Development Studies and Security Studies.

(a) The Concept of Human Security

Human insecurity is, of course, nothing new to humanity. Human beings have long suffered from the effects of drought, famine, disease, for instance. As Sabina Alkire explains, "[w]hat has changed, and changed considerably, are the kinds of insecurity people face, and the institutional possibilities of tempering that insecurity."[41]

Human security calls into question the primacy of national security by arguing that the principal referent object of security should be the individual rather than the state. Proponents of human security argue that a people-centered view of security is necessary in order to achieve national, regional, and global security.

The concept of human security appeared within both academic and policy arenas. In the academic arena, the concept emerged from Critical Security Studies (CSS), with the publication of Ken Booth's 1991 article "Security and Emancipation."[42] Traditionally, security was thought to come from citizenship.[43] One of the concerns of the CSS approach to human security was that the state can sometimes be the cause of insecurity rather than the provider of security.[44] Concentrating on national security was, thus, not enough to ensure the security of individuals.

The concept of human security represents a more significant break with the state-centrism of the realist security paradigm than was achieved by the Copenhagen School – a major contributor to the widening of Security Studies. While the sectoral approach of Buzan, Waever, and de Wilde allowed for something other than the state to be a referent object of security, only the state was viewed as having the capacity to decide whether something could be acted on as a matter of urgency. To this end, the primacy of the state was not entirely avoided.[45]

In the policy arena, the concept of human security was defined and employed primarily within the context of the UN system.[46] As mentioned, the United Nations Development Programme's 1994 Human Development Report, *New Dimensions of Human Security*, is considered a milestone publication in the development of the concept of human security. Broadly speaking, it defined human security as comprising freedom from fear and freedom from want.[47] This means that security implies the absence of hunger and illness, respect for human rights and dignity, as well as the absence of violence and armed conflict, which inflict huge suffering on civilian populations. The report presents seven elements of human security: economic, food, health, environmental, personal, community, and political security.[48]

While the concept of human security is relatively new, the security of individuals has, of course, been promoted for some time through a series of interconnected multilateral agreements, through international organizations, as well as through the voluntary sector. The Red Cross has also been concerned with individual security since the 19th century, and the Geneva Conventions, which materialized in the wake of World War II, established norms for the humane treatment of civilians in time of war. The UN has also championed human rights, which constitute an important element of human security, and has made a substantial contribution to the development of international human rights law. Both the UN Charter and the 1948 Universal Declaration of Human Rights are prime examples of this.

In addition, international aid and development assistance have made, and continue to make, a significant contribution to the promotion of human security. Emergency humanitarian relief has always been primarily concerned with the well-being of people. People's basic needs have always been its primary concern in the midst of crisis. Development assistance has complemented humanitarian aid by attempting to build sustainable economies as well as by strengthening the capacity of developing countries to manage both internal and external security issues.

More recently, a number of states have also been ardent proponents of human security. South Africa was one of the earliest subscribers to the concept and practice of human security. Japan also sought to make human security a central part of its foreign-policy agenda in the late 1990s and established a Trust for Human Security.[49] In Canada, in particular, human security has become an important part of foreign policy that grew out of a desire to engage in soft security practices. Canadians have been pioneers in the effort to ban the use of landmines, and the Canadian government signed a declaration with the Norwegian government at the 1998 Lysoen Conference that launched the Human Security Network. This network advocates global policies centered on human interests.[50] In 2007, the network comprised Austria, Canada, Chile, Costa Rica, Greece, Ireland, Jordan, Mali, the Netherlands, Slovenia, Switzerland, and Thailand, and South Africa is also an observer.[51]

The concept of human security was also endorsed in September 2004 by the European Union in its Barcelona Report of the Study Group on Europe's Security Capabilities, entitled *A Human Security Doctrine for Europe*. In the publication, the study group called for a human-security response force. Such a force would have a significant civilian component and even the military component would be heavily informed by the concept of human security.

That said, no one agreed-upon concept of human security exists.[52] While its inclusiveness has opened it up to the criticism that it exposes Security Studies to too many concerns, potentially diluting it, it remains attractive because it captures the multifarious factors that contribute to individual insecurity.[53]

Despite the fact that the concept of human security challenged the traditional focus on national security in security thinking, it is, however, not entirely independent from the state and in many ways dependent on it. As Mike Fell notes, human security is not incompatible with state security, but complementary to it. Indeed, "[h]uman security works with other types of security, whilst simultaneously attempting to adapt the policies of other types of security....states and 'security studies' are not withering away, but renegotiating and reshaping the security agenda."[54]

A number of threats to human security are transnational in nature, such as organized criminal networks that span state territorial borders, the traffic of drugs and small arms and light weapons (SALW), and some effects of environmental degradation. The latter example is indicative of the linkage between human and environmental security. Other threats to human security, such as the violation of human rights are interlinked with transcultural security.

(b) Threats to Human Security

By focusing on the individual, human security helps to reveal the interconnections between diverse security concerns. Conflicts may, for example, involve ethnic animosities, the use of small arms purchased at low cost, paramilitaries and mercenaries, and the use of child soldiers, and they may also be partly funded through local and international organized crime.[55]

The processes of globalization have also arguably intensified human insecurity. Many new threats are emerging and some old threats are being intensified as the pace of globalization accelerates, outpacing the capacity of governments to develop policy responses. Existing systems and protection mechanisms are fast becoming inadequate to tackle the human insecurities faced by people today. Public policy could do more to favor the positive effects of globalizing processes. Such policies require action by national governments, international cooperation, and global solidarity.[56]

(i) Human Mobility

Today, a combination of decolonization, the collapse of communist regimes, demographic imbalances, and global economic processes has increased human mobility and, consequently, the number of international migrants globally. We, indeed, live in a period of mass migration. Human mobility has, of course, always taken place for reasons specific to particular historical periods, with associated insecurities. Wars, slavery, economic crises, mercantile monopolies have all caused people to go on the move before.[57]

According to Robert Bach, what characterizes the current era of mass migration is not its overall volume: The global economic boom of the 19th century generated a large number of international migrants. In his view, global migration of today is characterized by the fact that it is shaped by deep structural inequalities in the global economy.[58]

As a result, the viability of existing immigration regimes is being challenged. States have reacted in a variety of ways to international migration. Some countries have taken a hard line on immigration, often in response to the use of illegal immigration as a political tool by right-wing politicians. One of the possible consequences of this is the illegal trafficking of people. Most of the victims of human trafficking are women and girls from poor countries and communities, who represent a profitable form of trade.

Having survived sometimes perilous journeys, many victims of human trafficking may find themselves in highly vulnerable situations. For example, many women entering countries illegally may find themselves working in the sex industry with little protection from middlemen or even police officers. In addition, these women are unlikely to receive support from society as a whole, which may view them as "expendable victims" of rape, physical violence, and even murder.[59]

While human trafficking constitutes a severe violation of human rights, legislation and strong enforcement mechanisms in receiving countries often do not help because the victims fall outside national legal frameworks. People's vulnerability to human trafficking is increased by the bureaucratic and time-consuming legal procedures that drive migrants to use illegal channels to cross borders. Corrupt government officials often collaborate with traffickers. Moreover, rather than being treated as victims, trafficked people are treated as criminals. Therefore, they fear arrest and detention if they contact local authorities or official representatives of their country of origin. This situation often results in perpetrators going unpunished and remaining anonymous.

In countries of origin, prevention should start with improved employment opportunities, better access to education, as well as enhanced representation in power structures. Transit and destination countries should focus on better border control and anti-corruption measures, non-criminalization of victims, institutionalization of protection programs, institutionalization of benefits, and access to witness protection in case of release. The need to come up with a clear definition of victims of trafficking in domestic legislation is also extremely urgent.[60]

(ii) Global Health Risks
Health issues have not been traditionally conceived as security concerns. Yet, health security is also becoming a major preoccupation in the context of globalization. At the most basic level, untimely death can be caused by human insecurity resulting from health risks. The tragedy is that many of these deaths may be preventable. A number of more specific linkages between health threats and human insecurity are noteworthy, such as conflict and violence, and the spread of infectious diseases.

An increased number of conflicts now occur within states rather than between them, and are often marked by a collapse of governance in the countries in question. These types of conflicts can involve the displacement of people, violations of human rights, genocide, and rape as a tool of war, for example. Violence leading to death and health problems is not, however, limited to times of war but may also be the result of crime and domestic violence.[61] Indeed, the most common form of violence that women experience is violence perpetrated by their intimate partners.[62]

The spread of infectious diseases also poses a serious human-security challenge. While illness is an age-old concern, greater human interaction – the result of increased migration and the transnationalization of production, markets, and services – exacerbates the problem and makes the task of preventing the spread of infectious disease even more challenging. Awareness about global health risks has been raised especially as a result of fears about the spread of HIV/AIDS and about bio-terrorism, which aims to create fear and undermine a society's confidence and resilience by increasing the sense of vulnerability.

As a result of their level of vulnerability and numerous deprivations, the impact of health risks on the poor is often acute. Ill-health may be a source of concern due to the implications that it may have on people's livelihoods and incomes. For people with little or no savings, emergency care or extended periods of hospitalization may result in impoverishment, the depletion of savings, or even a lack of treatment. This is, of course, likely to be particularly worrisome in countries where there is little or no publicly funded primary healthcare treatment.

The ramifications of global infectious diseases can be devastating. In order to prevent a disease from spreading to other countries, a country may, for instance, face restrictions on exports or a reduction of tourism in countries dependent on revenues from the tourist industry, which may cause people to lose their livelihoods.[63] The implications of such developments can have a negative impact on a state's economic security.

Rather than focusing on overall health improvement, a human-security approach places emphasis on the protection of people and their empowerment, so that they may better protect themselves.

(iii) Global Crime
Crime represents a threat to the lives of ordinary people in every country. The challenges that states face in relation to crime prevention have, however, increased in recent years. Organized criminal networks have been some of the most entrepreneurial actors in exploiting the opportunities created by the processes and technologies associated with globalization. Criminal syndicates have expanded their activities across borders, building transnational networks, using open economic and political borders for an array of activities, including the traffic of drugs, arms, and human beings, as well as money laundering.

The spread of crime exposes people, *inter alia*, to threats to personal security as a result of drugs-related crime, for example. The illegal trafficking of SALW can also prolong conflicts in which civilians may be deeply affected,[64] as well as leave weapons in circulation well after a conflict is over. SALW, are therefore, an important threat to human security, as well as to state sovereignty and state institutions in some countries.[65]

The risks posed by global crime to individuals are likely to be particularly acute in states that lack the necessary organized political authority with which to maintain public order or even to control large areas of state territory. In such states, people may live in an environment that is effectively in a permanent state of lawlessness. Afghanistan is an oft-cited example of a "failed state." After its invasion by the Soviet Union in 1979, Afghanistan found itself at the epicenter of a proxy war between the Soviet Union and the United States (US), with the US providing assistance to the *mujaheddin* resistance fighters. The end of the Cold War did not, however, mark the end of the conflict in Afghanistan. Rival factions struggled for power in the vacuum that followed the superpower pullout. One consequence of this situation has been the rise of Afghanistan's heroin industry. Indeed, the Taliban regime that gained control of the country in 1996 used the revenues gained from selling heroin to attempt to bolster the country's economy.[66]

(iv) Instability of Financial Markets
The growth of financial flows and the instability of financial markets generated by deregulation are also a source of human insecurity. This is especially the case in developing countries. Capital flows to developing countries tend to be characterized by a greater degree of volatility than those to developed countries.

As Stephany Griffith-Jones and Jenny Kimmis note, "[f]rom a human security and development perspective, the international financial system should deliver sufficient and sufficiently stable private and public funds to sustain more rapid growth and more investment than would otherwise take place in different developing countries."[67] Yet, the reality can be very different. In the early 1990s, many developing countries attracted considerable amounts of financial capital. Initially, this helped to boost growth. However, it also led to the overvaluation of currencies and created a current-account deficit as exports became increasingly expensive. This left many developing countries extremely vulnerable to the effect of a decline in confidence among international investors. In such situations, when investors withdraw large amounts of capital, the exchange rate collapses, the banking system comes under pressure and may even collapse, economic activity slows down, and job losses ensue.[68]

The 1997 East Asian financial crisis, for example, destabilized millions of lives and negatively affected the growth prospects in that region and in the world for several years. The human-security impact of the crisis was severe in Indonesia, South Korea, Malaysia, the Philippines, and Thailand. The human-security toll included the loss of capital, job losses, healthcare crises, increases in the cost of food and essentials, an increase in the number of suicides, higher rates of domestic violence, more school drop-outs, and a reduction in school attendance. The poor, especially in rural areas, were particularly badly affected.[69]

Financial crises in developing countries can develop into economic crises. Such crises not only increase poverty in the short term but also affect growth prospects over the long run as a result of falling investment and job creation. Central banks often pursue tight monetary policies leading to high interest rates following financial crises, which can discourage investment. In addition, governments may also reduce spending in order to decrease fiscal deficits or to generate financial surpluses. The poorest in society are likely to be impacted by such measures, since they tend to be more dependent on state welfare.[70]

Those calling for reform argue that governance structures at the national, regional, and global level are required to better manage economic and financial integration, as well as reform of the global financial system. Increased transparency and better regulation of international loans, for example, would help to reduce the impact of instabilities in financial markets. Effective regulation would require consistency in its application, a global regulatory authority or, alternatively, increased exchange of information and coordination between national regulatory authorities.[71]

(v) Labor-Market Instabilities
The transnationalization of production and services, the competition for global markets, and rapid technological changes all create new opportunities for jobs. Nonetheless, they are also associated with increasingly flexible labor markets and job insecurity. With high levels of competition in rapidly changing market environments, workers are required to take on new activities, to train, and even retrain, as employers lay off and hire new workers. Within this context, perhaps the greatest threats to human security come not from high levels of unemployment, but from the ever present threat of corporate restructuring and downsizing that inevitably lead to redundancies. Indeed, insecurity as a result of this precarious situation has been further intensified in many countries as worker-dismissal laws have been weakened. Temporary workers today represent a considerable proportion of the global workforce. In some countries, the informal sector is also growing to absorb formally unemployed people.[72]

(vi) Poverty, Conflict, and Development
Poor people tend to be particularly vulnerable to security risks of various kinds. Current trends suggest, for example, persistent and worsening food insecurity for many people in the developing world.[73] They are also often the most affected by physical forms of violence and crime.

Inequality as a source of human insecurity is a matter of disparities not only in terms of wealth, but also in terms of political participation (in parliaments, cabinets, armies, and local governments), resources (in land, human capital, and communal resources), and social conditions (in education, housing, and employment). The uneven nature of globalization thus has the potential to create tension and conflicts within communities, states, and regions, which inevitably have an impact on human security.

In situations of conflict, people may be at risk due to reduced access to the basic means of survival, such as water, food, and shelter, as well as due to violence. Women and girls are particularly vulnerable to sexual violence during conflicts, taking the form, for example, of rape, forced pregnancy, forced prostitution, forced sterilization, trafficking, and indecent assault. Indeed, in some recent conflicts rape has been used as a means of waging war.[74]

Children are especially vulnerable in times of conflict. They may suffer as a result of displacement, sexual exploitation, separation from their families, abduction, or of being used as soldiers. Some may become street children as a result of conflict. The experiences of children in conflict are likely to be different from those of adults, and the psychological and physical scars are likely to be profound.[75]

In addition, inadequate attention to individual well-being in post-conflict reconstruction activities can compromise the chances of success in rebuilding communities. If people's economic needs, physical security, and individual rights do not form an adequate part of post-conflict reconstruction efforts, human insecurity can outlast the conflict itself, perhaps leading to renewed tensions.[76]

(c) Achievements and Challenges

Axworthy notes that, "Despite how quickly the concept has been validated, getting states to practice human security remains a difficult and uneven process."[77] The problem is one of wrong focus, since promoting human security complements and enhances national security. Focusing on human security helps one to discern the complex relationship between various security challenges and highlights the need to address them simultaneously. It captures, for example, numerous insecurities related to the failure to meet basic economic and social needs, as well as those related to conflict. At the state level, policy makers face the challenge of creating competitive market conditions while ensuring that this also enhances individual well-being. In relation to domestic labor markets, most governments have been more responsive to employers' demands for a more flexible labor force, and alternative forms of social protection have been slow to develop.[78]

Thus, one major obstacle to developing state practices that enhance human security is the dominance of narrow conceptions of national interest. Axworthy notes that:

> We have witnessed failures, back-filling, and hesitancy to act in favor of defenseless people... The campaign to end repression of ethnic Albanians by the Milosevic regime was a serious test of both international will and readiness to turn the talk of protecting people into concrete action. For the most part we passed. The North Atlantic Treaty Organization (NATO) reversed the ethnic cleansing practice and saved the lives of untold numbers of people. But the

Kosovo experience left some troubling questions about the willingness of the members of the UN Security Council to place international peace and security above individual national interests.

Intervention to end the suffering of hundreds and thousands of ethnic Albanians should have had Security Council authorization from the outset. It did not.[79]

Moreover, subsequent events in East Timor, Sierra Leone, and the Democratic Republic of the Congo, which required the international community to act, were also surrounded by uncertainty, with the void being filled by individual countries or regional groupings, where they existed. Indeed, one of the challenges at the regional level is to construct effective crisis-management forces.

Weaknesses also exist in post-conflict situations in which the UN and other organizations are expected to engage in reconstruction. These organizations often lack the experience to adequately deal with such problems. Canada has made some significant progress in this area insofar as it is making an effort to focus on how to reconstruct communities. For example, over a period of two years, Canada has devoted more than $220 million to peace-building initiatives in Kosovo, with particular emphasis on education, corrections, and police services. In Sierra Leone, Canada has focused on the rehabilitation of combatants, especially child soldiers. And, in Haiti, it has focused its efforts on the rehabilitation of the justice system.[80]

Globally, human security renders visible the interrelationship between poverty, violent conflict, and inequality. It therefore highlights that these three areas need to be addressed together in order to be effective. Despite this, they tend to be dealt with separately, which has created gaps. According to Sakiko Fukuda-Parr, this is especially discernable between conflict resolution, humanitarian relief, and development. Conflict resolution focuses on political issues, humanitarian relief for people, and development on social and economic aspects. Multinational institutions need to give higher priority to the human-security perspective because it offers a more comprehensive view of people's well-being.[81] One of the problems facing multilateral institutions and the instruments that exist to protect human security, such as the Ottawa Convention (banning antipersonnel landmines), the International Criminal Court, and the Optional Protocol to the Convention on the Rights of the Child, is that they all rely on the cooperation of states while at the same time undermining traditional notions of sovereignty. Indeed, many recent international agreements that take individual well-being as their primary concern fundamentally impact the (traditionally perceived) internal sphere of states.

The logic of economic liberalization does not favor urgent responses to combat the spread of infectious diseases, though the technology exists. Strong profit incentives provide the motivation for investments in research and development of treatment and cures. Yet, these very same motives restrict access to those who have the necessary purchasing power. A tiny proportion of those suffering from HIV/AIDS currently have access to retroviral therapy, largely because of the costs of drugs and their protection under legislation on intellectual-property rights. In addition to the emergence of such new diseases, old diseases are reappearing or simply going unaddressed. For instance, while diseases like tuberculosis and malaria can be treated, they continue to kill millions every year because of a simple lack of access to the necessary treatment.[82] The duration of patents on new medicines should be reviewed and increased availability of generic medicines should be pursued.[83]

Indeed, since human security implies, among other things, freedom from hunger, disease, crime, and repression, it cannot be achieved in the absence of good governance at all levels.[84] Increasing personal security, for instance, through a sustained effort to reduce criminal activities requires not only state action, but also transnational cooperation at the regional and global levels. In order for transnational cooperation to adequately address these problems, good governance is required at all levels to ensure access to resources, protection of people's rights, representation, and social justice, etc. Yet, even in some of the most mature democracies, governance structures are inadequate. At the regional level, where they exist, they tend to be only embryonic at best. And, at the global level, as mentioned, the primacy of international law is not respected as it should be, and multilateral institutions are frequently at the mercy of the geopolitical interests of large states, and the scope of both international law and multilateral institutions is not as wide as it should be in order to further the security of the individual.

3. Environmental Security

While the environment has more readily been perceived as a developmental or conservational concern, its relevance to security and stability is increasingly being acknowledged. In some instances, the notion of environmental security is associated with the intrinsic value of the biosphere itself. In other cases, as indicated the implications of environmental insecurity on human security has been stressed. In others, its impact on national security has been emphasized. For example, with the increasing number of natural disasters and large-scale operations required to deal with the impact of such events, the costs to a national budget and perhaps the state's legitimacy are high. There is also an increasing awareness of the interrelationship between the environment and global political and economic factors. Following Hurricane Katrina, for example, the price of oil rose sharply as another potential hurricane in the Gulf of Mexico was predicted in 2005.[85] The subsequent drop in production had a sizable impact on the global economy. The sense in which the impact of environmental insecurity may affect a number of countries at once is also evident in instances of air or water pollution, for example. This illustrates the interconnection between environmental and transnational security.

(a) The Concept and Its Emergence
Concerns about the environment have traditionally been associated with development and conservation. More recently, with worries over the impact of global environmental change, the environment has increasingly become identified as a security concern. While the interrelationship between the environment and other societal facets is nothing new,[86] the connection between environmental change and security is often recognized as having been made in the 1970s. At this time, the environment was identified as a security issue because of its potential to generate more traditional national-security concerns, including violent conflict and tension.[87] With the end of the Cold War, environmental change increasingly became acknowledged within Environmental and Security Studies as a security matter concerning both states and people. Parallel to these developments, environmental concerns were also making their way onto international political and policy agendas.[88]

The global implications of environmental security have been viewed in a variety of ways. As mentioned, many interpretations of environmental security focus on the manner in which environmental change may impact upon national security. This is largely due to the dominance of state-centric thinking in academic and policy circles. When the primary referent object of security is assumed to be the state, environmental security may affect national security in a number of ways. Given that sovereignty over specified territory is the material substrata of national security, environmental change may seriously affect national security by causing a rise in sea level, for example, which may reduce a state's territory, as well as displace a significant quantity of its population. Climate change may also affect national security by reducing state legitimacy or national economic growth. Finally, given the dominant concern of national-security policy makers with violent conflict and transborder incursions, the issue of whether and how climate change may be linked to the outbreak of conflicts or a surge in migration may also be considered important.[89]

Alternative referent objects of security, such as individuals, are also increasingly being considered in relation to environmental security. Here, the concern is with individual well-being. Environmental change may negatively impact on individual well-being by reducing crop yields and the availability of fresh water, destroying livelihoods, or exposing people to new diseases, and it may also interact with a number of other factors that may generate tension and violent conflict.

In addition to being considered in relation to the state and individual well-being, the referent object of environmental security may also be understood to be the physical and biological components of the natural world. As the source from which resources such as water, air, minerals, and other critical elements are derived, the environment enables all human activity.[90] Moreover, environmental security is not simply concerned with conflicts and shortages for people, it embraces the natural world and its processes, some of which are interconnected with human activities.[91]

As Buzan, Waever, and de Wilde point out, discussions of environmental security that focus on the impact of human activity on the biosphere are often fundamentally concerned with the maintenance of attained levels of civilization rather than the biosphere itself. This implies that the referent object of security is the current level of civilization: "The concern in all cases is whether the ecosystems that are crucial to preserve (or further develop) the achieved level of civilization are sustainable."[92] They argue that environmental security concerns the maintenance of local and planetary biospheres as the support system of all other human enterprises.

Some threats from human activity to natural systems or structures of the planet do not seem to pose threats to the existence of (parts of) civilization. Obvious examples are, at the global level, greenhouse-gas emissions and the effects of chlorofluorocarbons (CFCs) and other industrial emissions on the ozone layer. At the regional and local levels, this relates to environmental exploitation (by extraction, dumping, or accidental destruction) beyond the capacity of smaller ecosystems, which upsets the economic base and social fabric of the states involved.

Yet, as Buzan, Waever, and de Wilde point out, some threats posed to the biosphere by human activity do not represent threats to current levels of civilization. The depletion of certain energy and mineral resources, for example, may cause human beings inconvenience but do not pose a threat to their survival. The implications of such depletion can be minimized by the creation of substitutes enabled by advances in technology. Another clear example is that of the extinction of particular animals.[93] For this reason, the biosphere and the current levels of civilization should both be considered as referent objects of environmental security, depending on the specific issue at hand.

While disputes have occurred over whether the environment itself or civilization should be identified as the referent object, consensus does exist about the fundamental problem. Not only is human enterprise conditioned by the environment, but it also conditions the environment itself. Instead of a one-way, linear relationship between structural environmental conditions and likely policy options, a dynamic, interdependent relationship exists between the environment and human activities: Civilization is held responsible for part of its own structural environmental conditions, which limit or enlarge its development options and influence incentives for conflict and cooperation.[94] In global terms, the interaction between the environment and civilization is the result of two developments: the explosive growth of both the world population and economic activity.

Environmental change on Earth is not unique to this particular period in history. However, what is specific to our time is the degree of change under way. Ecosystems have never before been altered with such intensity. While some changes are specific to the 20th century, notably the thinning of the ozone layer, most are linked to the intensity and scale of human activities that interact with the environment.[95] To be sure, humans have been felling timber, mining ore, producing waste, raising crops, and hunting animals for centuries, but we had been doing so much less intensively up to the post-World War II era.

Most of the activities that we engage in that risk altering the environment are economic in nature. According to J.R. McNeil, in his book *Something New Under the Sun: An Environmental History of the Twentieth-Century World*, the world economy in the latter part of the 20th century was some 120 times larger than it was in 1500, with the majority of this growth occurring after 1820. Moreover, the growth rate during the post-World War II period has been unprecedented in human history.[96]

A vast majority of this growth has been driven by population increase, and the rest has been due to technological and organizational innovations. Since the agricultural revolution around 8000 BC, the human population has expanded considerably. Since the 18th century, it has grown extremely quickly compared to previous rates. Since 1950, the world population has been growing approximately 10,000 times faster than it did before the invention of agriculture.[97]

The Industrial Revolution, in particular, brought about a tremendous change in the interaction between human activity and the environment, due to accompanying advances in technology. It enabled the conversion of biomass energy stocks into mechanical power.[98] According to McNeil, "No other century – no millennium – in human history can compare with the twentieth for its growth in energy use."[99] Of course, with industrialization came air pollution. The specificity of our time is linked to the long period of economic growth in which we are living. One consequence of this is that, "The human species has shattered the constraints and rough stability of the old economic, demographic, and energy regimes."[100]

The notion of population concentration and economic activity straining the capacity of biospheres to maintain the well-being of a population is relevant not only at the global level, but at all levels of analysis. Urbanization, for example, is usually associated with local problems of overpopulation, pollution is typically related to local industrial problems, and soil erosion is often linked to low-level economic and population pressures.

As Buzan, Waever, and de Wilde point out, whenever the environment is raised to the level of a security issue, some level of human responsibility is implied. Indeed, the central idea behind environmental security is that human beings are generating environmental changes that pose risks to their own future as well as that of other species. In other words, the patterns of consumption of human beings are outstripping the Earth's capacities to support them without those capacities undergoing degradation. These patterns of consumption involve several variables, such as total population, production modes, and gross per capita consumption levels. In short, carrying capacity depends on population size, technology, and lifestyle choices.[101]

Crucial to understanding environmental security is the idea that it is possible to reverse this trend. The problem is one of mankind's struggle not with nature but with the dynamics of its own cultures – a civilizational issue that is largely linked to economic and demographic developments, and that has potential implications for degrees of order in the international system and its subsystems.[102]

(b) Threats to Environmental Security

Environmental security encompasses a gamut of challenges, such as global climate change, water and air pollution, and the degradation of scarce resources. It may lead to the increased severity of natural disasters, inflict severe economic harm, destabilize societies, and even contribute to interstate and intrastate conflicts.[103] At the most fundamental level, environmental damage and degradation affects human security. Disease caused by water pollution is perhaps one of the most elementary examples of the connection between the environment and human security. Another source of human insecurity linked to environmental damage or degradation is damage to livelihoods. In the latter case, environmental security may overlap with economic security.

(i) Deforestation and the Threat to Biodiversity

Ecosystems can be disrupted by a number of causes, such as deforestation. Forests are essential to life on Earth. They determine the continuity and stability of major biogeochemical cycles. Forests cover 40 percent of the world's terrestrial surface and constitute a haven for 80 percent of the world's biodiversity. They are also critical to the creation and maintenance of freshwater flows. Moreover, they are the key to atmospheric maintenance, and, as a result, have become central in international debates about climate change, greenhouse-gas emissions, and carbon eradication.[104]

The 20th century has seen roughly 50 percent of the Earth's original forests cleared, fragmented, or otherwise spoiled.[105] Large-scale degradation of landscape and accompanying damage to forest resources has resulted in significant disruption to watersheds. Water quality has also been reduced and aquatic organisms have disappeared.[106]

Alterations to forest ecosystems are frequently overlooked due to their lack of visibility on satellite images. Global calculations against deforestation carried out by the UN Food and Agricultural Organization give an accurate picture of degradation of forest ecosystems where forest cover still exists. The impact of deforestation on other ecological aspects of forests are often referred to as "cryptic deforestation," which is caused by numerous factors, including ground fires, increased poaching, defaunation, mining, poor forest management, and overgrazing. Resulting changes in sub-canopy structures negatively affect the functions of forest ecosystems, which include the provision of habitat for tropical migratory birds in the Americas.[107]

Loss and fragmentation of forests may also be facilitating the spread of disease. For instance, increases in malaria and leishmaniasis are partly due to habitat changes resulting from deforestation: The new habitats being created are promoting disease-carrying insects. Pathogens are increasing across all ecosystems, including oceans and aquatic ecosystems. Episodes of toxic algae blooms have increased, and there is increasing transport of cholera, as well as development of conditions for drug-resistant variants. The emergence of thirty or so new diseases over the last fifteen years is viewed as evidence of the increasingly heavy impact of human activity on ecosystems, aiding the ability of emerging diseases to evolve in step, maximizing the impact on people and perhaps other species as well.[108]

Deforestation is also resulting in a loss of biodiversity, which refers to the huge diversity of plant and animal species that make up the planet's local, regional, and global ecosystems. As a result of humans' disruption of ecosystems, a large number of species are already extinct and others may soon become so. Their extinction is partly the result of overhunting and overfishing, as well as the introduction of non-native species that crowd native species out. Yet, one of the greatest causes of the extinction of animal and plant species is the loss of habitat resulting from deforestation, as well as water pollution and increased urbanization.[109] The diversity of birds, for instance, is being reduced as a result of the felling of timber and other human activity. As a result, the ecosystem services provided by birds, including control of insect populations, are also consequently being reduced.

(ii) Water Scarcity
As Helga Haftendorn has aptly put it, "water is the foundation of human life, is a finite and scarce resource, and is a common and divided

resource."[110] As states industrialize, the requirement for water increases as a result of more extensive agricultural activity and population growth. Water supplies are, however, becoming depleted in some areas. By the mid-1990s, 80 countries, representing 40 percent of the world's population, suffered serious water shortages.[111]

Unsafe drinking water and inadequate sanitation also present a problem. Both increase the spread of water-born diseases, such as malaria and diarrhea, hepatitis A and E, and cholera. Ensuring safe, reliable, and reasonably priced water and sanitation presents an ongoing challenge. At present, many people still lack access to clean water and basic sanitation. In addition, the cost-effectiveness of policies and activities aimed at water-quality management is poor.

Moreover, since poor water quality can often lead to diarrhea, inadequate water-quality management can also be an indirect cause of malnutrition. Ill-health can, in turn, affect people's capacity to engage in productive economic activity, which can ultimately pose a significant problem for a country's capacity to sustain economic growth. This situation represents a major threat to achieving sustainable development.[112] Thus, inadequate water-quality management and water allocation represent a threat not only to human security, but also to the economic security of developing countries.

Due to its scarcity, its necessity for life and good health, and for sustained development, fresh water is likely to be a source of insecurity, tension, and perhaps conflict in the coming decades.[113] Since water supplies, including rivers and water tables, cross international boundaries, the result can be tension and conflict.[114] The highly publicized dispute between Mexico and the US over transboundary water management is a case in point.[115] But water conflict is, of course, not limited to this region. In fact, it is increasing in many parts of the world, including the Nile Basin, the Jordan Basin, and the Ganges Basin,[116] often in relation to scarcity or pollution. It can be local, as well as regional. As populations increase, conflicts over the distribution of water resources among different sectors, as well as between different groups, are likely to increase. Yet, environmental security represents a challenge not only at the domestic level, but also at the transnational level since the impact of environmental damage or degradation can affect a number of countries. Environmental issues can, therefore, also become state-level security issues. In many of the cases of environmentally induced conflicts, migration and subsequent tensions have played a significant role.[117]

(iii) Global Climate Change
Global climate change refers to a slow, long-term change in the Earth's temperature. While the scientific evidence for global climate change is disputed, most scientists suggest that world temperature is likely to increase by between 2 and 9 degrees over the next fifty years. Climate change, however, implies more than rising temperatures. Polar ice caps have already begun to melt and sea levels are likely to rise.[118] Rising sea levels are already beginning to affect islands in the Pacific Ocean, where the evacuation of entire populations is already being considered. Rising oceans also affect storm surges and tides, wind waves, and coastal currents.[119]

There are also likely to be changes in the amount of rainfall and snowfall, in evaporation rates, and in the amount of water run-off into rivers and lakes. Heavy rains and snowstorms in higher altitudes may become more frequent. Intense hurricanes and cyclones like those that hit Florida and the Caribbean over the last ten years could become more common. Agricultural regions in Africa, Asia, and North America may experience droughts and severe heat waves. Shifts in the Gulf Stream may make northern Europe much colder.

The potential biological ramifications of global climate change are omnipresent, though as yet uncertain. Organisms ranging from trees to coral reefs to mosquitoes are sensitive to changes in climate. In some regions of the world, wetter weather, a longer growing season, and more carbon dioxide in the atmosphere may be good for agricultural yields. At the same time, increased evaporation of water from the soil, heavier rainfall, and pest-hospitable weather may increase climate-related agricultural risks. Other regions may experience changes in agriculture and food security of a different order. If rainy seasons do not occur or are highly unpredictable, this may result in droughts, food shortages, and famines.[120]

Environmental damage may also increase the severity of natural disasters. The impact of natural disasters, such as the tsunami in the Indian Ocean, the earthquake in Pakistan, and Hurricane Katrina, is relevant to both human and transnational security. Natural disasters affect individuals at the most basic level, killing and maiming, leaving them homeless, displacing them, devastating livelihoods, and disrupting healthcare services, clean water supplies, and adequate housing facilities. Moreover, particular segments of the population may be disproportionately affected by natural disasters,[121] such as women, children, the elderly, the disabled, and the poor.

Natural disasters can also make communities more vulnerable in the future by, for example, devastating or disrupting local ecosystems. In addition, at the state level, the damage to infrastructure and the disruption of productive activity can pose significant economic problems. Natural disasters take an enormous toll on development. They can even put at risk some countries' capacity for development. Yet, sometimes, natural disasters are the result of regretful development strategies. The development choices made by individuals, communities, and states can increase the risks related to natural disasters, as well as their distribution among the population of affected countries. Ill-conceived development projects are also partly to blame for damage to infrastructure as a result of floods.[122]

Africa, in particular, is thought to be most vulnerable to the impact of global climate change, largely due to reductions in water availability, enhanced food security and flooding, negative health effects, and increased desertification. Asia is also likely to suffer from problems of food security and flooding. Latin America may also experience increasingly severe and perhaps more frequent climatic variations as a result of changes in the El Nino Southern Oscillation, as well as decreasing biodiversity and reduced crop yields. The most severely affected developing countries are, however, likely to be small island states.[123]

(iv) Ozone Depletion
A second major atmospheric problem is the depletion of the ozone layer. Ozone high in the atmosphere filters harmful ultraviolet rays from the sun. Certain chemicals used in industrial production interact with ozone in a manner that breaks it down. As the ozone layer is depleted, a higher degree of ultraviolet radiation is reaching the Earth's surface. The ozone layer is thinnest over Antarctica. A thinning of the ozone layer was also detected over North America in the 1990s. Over the long run, ozone depletion could have environmental consequences. Increased radiation could kill vegetation, reduce agricultural yields, and disrupt ecosystems. The impact on human well-being is already being felt, as ozone depletion is increasing the risks of skin cancer.[124] In addition, many epidemiology studies suggest a positive association between levels of ozone and respiratory conditions, diminished lung function, and a variety of other health problems. A recent, but growing, body of literature also suggests increased mortality in large cities.[125]

(c) Achievements and Challenges

Simon Dalby, a leading proponent of environmental security, argues that:

> The assumption that the environment is separate from both humanity and economic systems lies at the heart of the policy difficulties facing sustainable development and security thinking. The ideas of the environment as an independent variable – something that is beyond human control and that stresses societies in ways that require a policy response – presents a problem for the environmental dimension of human security. As the burgeoning environmental history literature makes abundantly clear, the sheer scale of human activity renders this assumption inadequate for both scholarship and policy formulation. Instead researchers and decision-makers should focus more specifically on ecology.[126]

To some extent, this has been taken on board by a number of actors. Buzan, Waever, and de Wilde point out that leading actors in the environmental sector tend to be particularly active in relation to specific issues in specific instances. Sometimes, these actors are states. Australia, for example, played a particularly important role in regime formation for Antarctica. Sweden and Norway have been strong promoters of international action on transboundary air pollution, particularly acid rain.[127]

A major impediment to addressing issues of environmental security are the often competing interests of domestic environmental lobbies and industrial business lobbies within states. The principal dilemmas here are related to short-term costs and long-term benefits and the fact that special interest groups, linked to oil companies and industry, pay the costs but are not the sole beneficiaries. The US case amply demonstrates these dilemmas. At issue is a conflict between short-term economic interests and long-term security interests.[128] Yet, it refuses to sign up to the Kyoto Protocol. The US case is interesting not only from this point of view, but also because of its influence on the global agenda.[129]

The challenge of environmental security is often a problem of governance and institutions. At one level, environmental crises are not just linked to environmental degradation and scarcity of resources, but also to the lack of, or inadequate nature of, environmental-management policies. As research on the situation in South Asia demonstrates, a lack of institutional or governance capacities often contributes to human insecurity resulting from a lack of scarce resources or the degradation of environmental resources.[130] Environmental degradation does not simply turn into conflict, but it may lead to conflict where there are inadequate means to address the problem.

Globally, the dilemma stems from the fact that the financial burdens of reversing the tide in relation to environmental degradation must be borne by states individually, but the benefits are shared more widely. This dilemma is further complicated by the North-South dimension. Many governments in the developing world argue that they should be able to industrialize in the same way as the industrialized countries of the global North did in the past. Yet, the question remains as to how the industrialization of these countries can be accommodated while at the same time reducing air pollution. This was, in fact, one of the objections to the 1997 Kyoto Protocol voiced by the US. The protocol adopted a complex formula for reducing greenhouse-gas emissions to 1990 levels in the North over the period of a decade. Countries in the global South were granted preferential treatment, since their level of emissions is considerably lower, with the exception of China and India. The US Congress objected to this and subsequently declared that it would not ratify the treaty. Therefore, global warming negotiations remained at a stalemate.[131] While the North-South factor does make multilateral negotiations more complex, it ought to be remembered that the US is the largest greenhouse-gas emitter; China, India, and perhaps also Brazil have simply tipped the balance.

While Kyoto Protocol was finally adopted in 1997, many of the details had still to be defined. The protocol outlined the major dimensions of the mechanisms and compliance system, but failed to specify how they would work in practice. Rules for its implementation have now, however, been established.[132]

States have been more successful in negotiating agreements and developing regimes to manage the ozone problem. In the 1987 Montreal Protocol, 22 states agreed to reduce the use of CFCs by 50 percent by 1998. In 1990, the timetable was speeded up and the number of signatories expanded: 81 states agreed to eliminate all CFCs by 2000. In 1992, as evidence of ozone depletion grew, the timetable was again accelerated, with major industrial states phasing out CFCs by 1995. The signatories also agreed in principle to establish a fund to help developing countries finance alternative refrigeration technologies free of CFCs. These countries were also granted until 2010 to phase out production. But with payments from rich countries lagging, and an emerging black market in CFCs making their production more profitable, it is unclear whether countries in the global South will be able to eliminate CFCs in the near future. By the mid-1990s, China was the world's leader in terms of CFC emissions, and the top 10 included Mexico, Brazil, Thailand, India, and Argentina.[133]

In relation to the scientific agenda, the leading actor is not the state but the global, environmental epistemic community that undertakes research on a wide range of environmental issues, promotes an agenda, and communicates that agenda to the public and the political elite. Yet, a difficulty in this area is the complexity of identifying the root causes of environmental degradation or damage, which include both natural trends and those induced by human beings. The scientific evidence linking carbon dioxide and other greenhouse gases to global climate change is also contested.[134] This presents a significant challenge to reaching an agreement on multilateral measures aimed at reducing emissions: Lack of scientific evidence was another issue cited by the US Congress as a reason for its non-ratification of the Kyoto Protocol. The actors in this realm also include activists; lobbying non-governmental organizations, such as Greenpeace and the World Wildlife Fund (WWF); and some intergovernmental organizations, such as the United Nations Environment Programme (UNEP).[135]

According to some estimates, progress toward the advancement of environmental security has faded in the face of security concerns that are perceived as more urgent, such as the fight against terrorism.[136] The EU continues, nevertheless, to take some progressive steps toward stemming environmental degradation. The EU's 2003 security strategy, titled *A Secure Europe in a Better World*,[137] recognizes that security is paramount for development and also identifies the roles played by environmental factors in cycles of conflict. In addition, it has made considerable efforts to upgrade its development policy. The EU also brought forward at Johannesburg two initiatives on water and energy supply that aim to enhance security for the developing world. Despite this, the US role is pivotal, though sorely lacking.[138]

4. National Security

States have traditionally constituted the primary referent object of security. The state is typically linked to the use of force by virtue of the principle of sovereignty. Internally, the state is the highest political authority and, as such, has the means to enforce order. This implies that it has a monopoly on the use of force. Externally, the sovereign state coexists with other sovereign states in the context of international anarchy tasked with enforcing order. National security, therefore, traditionally encompasses a military and police dimension. The capacity to maintain order internally also implies the ability to avert internal challenges to state authority. Thus, national security also has political, economic, and societal components that are crucial for maintaining the legitimacy required to produce a stable institutionalized authority.

(a) Military
The traditional concept of sovereignty implies the exclusive right to self-government over a specified territory and population. Because force is particularly effective as a way of acquiring and controlling territory, the military is perceived as a particularly important dimension of national security. Historically, an important criterion ensuring the right to govern has been the capacity to assert and defend that claim against potential challengers both from within and without. Military threats and vulnerabilities have traditionally been accorded primacy in national-security thinking. This is because such challenges are usually intentional and they represent a breakdown of regular forms of communication and conflict resolution. While a body of international law has been developed and is continually expanding in part with the aim of channeling the use of armed force, its interpretation and application are sometimes fragile.

Indeed, military-security matters have traditionally arisen as means for ensuring the external and internal processes by which the machineries of government are maintained. Most states have progressively disarmed their citizenry and, historically, there has been a tendency toward an ideal in which the state is the only legitimate wielder of force in society and is able to more adequately protect a populace than any other armed group. One notable exception is the US, which grants its citizens the right to bear arms. Switzerland, Israel, and South Africa also retain strong elements of armed citizenry, the former linked to territorial defense and the latter two to individual security.[139]

Correspondingly, threats against which military responses may be employed may originate inside or outside the state. In instances where the perceived threat comes from within the state, military security tends to largely concern a ruling elite's maintenance of civil peace, territorial integrity, and, more controversially, the machinery of government in the face of challenges from its citizens. Typically, the latter challenges are militant separatist, revolutionary, terrorist, or criminal in character, although some governments may also identify unarmed challengers as threats to national security in order to enable the use of armed force against them.[140] Indeed, the military-security agenda revolves largely around the ability of governments to stem non-military threats to their existence, such as migrants and rival ideologies. This is manifest in the militarization of border controls in Europe, for example. According to Derek Lutterbeck, increased concern in European countries with irregular migration has resulted in greater militarization of migration control in the Mediterranean region. Militarization of border controls, in this case, involves the use of semi-military and military forces and hardware in an effort to prevent migration by sea.[141] In addition, the state also has challengers that have no aspiration to replace it or to seek the status of states.

Today, while states in Western Europe face little in the way of military threats, they nevertheless maintain substantial armed forces. However, these forces are often used for activities that that are no longer linked to a state's self-defense against aggression. States now put their militaries at the service of the international community. They have been used in consent-based peacekeeping missions, which are now viewed as "traditional" peace operations.

With the end of the Cold War, the rise of intrastate conflicts, the partial redefinition of sovereignty, and the practice of military intervention, militaries are regularly engaged in peace operations in response to crisis situations, as well as their aftermath. Peace operations involve four core activities: conflict prevention, peacemaking, peacekeeping, and peacebuilding. Militaries may be deployed for purposes far different from those of defending state territory. They may, for example, be deployed to help police a ceasefire or to support efforts to help establish state institutions. The evolution of the role of the military has been radically altered in a remarkably short period of time.[142]

(b) Political
Buzan, Waever, and de Wilde define political security as referring to the organizational stability of social orders. In other words, it implies the stability of institutionalized authority. While political security is often difficult to distinguish as a distinct subset of national security, some threats may have an overriding political dimension and do not employ significant military, identificational, economic, or environ-

mental means.[143] Perceptions of threats to political security generally emanate from challenges to traditional notions of state sovereignty. At the state level, threats may be posed by sub-state actors. According to Buzan, political security concerns a number of threats ranging from pressuring the government in relation to a specific policy, to secessionism, and disruption of the political fabric of the state so as to weaken it before a military attack.[144]

Political threats may be posed to a) the internal legitimacy of political units, which relates largely to ideologies and other constitutive ideas; and b) their external legitimacy. Threats from outside are not necessarily directed at sovereignty but can be aimed at a state's ideological legitimacy, that is, its domestic pillar, e.g., the Cold War. In the post-decolonization world, issues of formal recognition are rare. Nevertheless, many states founded on a more traditional notion of sovereignty may also view outside interventions of various kinds as threats to their political security.

Governments may be tempted to use security arguments when their concern is actually with their own self-preservation. This can be the case in relation to both external and internal threats. In a weak state, the authority of the regime as such is contested to a much greater degree than in strong states, where the framework and some basic legitimacy of the regime are generally accepted. In weak states, basic institutions and ideologies can easily be challenged. Political violence may be extensive; therefore, the power-holders try to make appeals in the name of the state. In such instances, many will view the government's action as taken on behalf of its own interests rather than those of the population. In a stronger state, especially a liberal-democratic one, there is a much stronger assumption that the government acts only as the legitimate agent of the state and that its claims are subject to public scrutiny and are open to question.

Buzan, Waever, and de Wilde approach the issue of threats and vulnerabilities through the argument that a state consists of three components: ideas, physical base, and institutions. Subtracting those issues that fall under other sectors, we are left with ideas (excluding identity) and institutions. It is all a question of the ideas that political institutions are built on. The ideas that hold a state together are usually nationalism (especially civic nationalism but sometimes ethnonationalism) and political ideology. By threatening these ideas, one can threaten the stability of a political order. Such threats might be to the existing structure of government, to the territorial integrity of the state (by encouraging defections from state identity), or to the existence of the state itself (by questioning its right to autonomy). Political threats take either the form of subversion of legitimacy or the denial of recognition (either total denial or denial of sovereign equality).

As indicated, the organizing concept for all of this is sovereignty. Threats to the existence of a state are those that ultimately involve sovereignty, because sovereignty is what defines the state as a state. Threats to state survival are, therefore, threats to sovereignty. Even minor violations may be viewed as threats, because sovereignty is a principle that claims the ultimate right of self-determination. External actors probably aim at less than sovereignty in their actions, but the logic of securitization means that the focus will, nevertheless, likely be sovereignty. During the Cold War, the West generally did not question the recognition of the Soviet Union as a sovereign state in the international system but aimed to weaken its domestic legitimacy. Nevertheless, governments claim not only to defend their political position but also their sovereignty in its external and internal dimensions.

A strong state will typically be invulnerable to a political threat. It will not be ethnically divided and thus not open to secessionist forces. Its government will neither be divorced from the general opinions of its citizens nor dependent upon suppressing views and information and therefore will be fairly invulnerable to external actors supporting oppositional voices. Such states may nevertheless feel politically threatened. During the Cold War, the US perceived both a political and a military threat from the Soviet Union in terms of the question of the legitimacy and efficiency of US democratic capitalism raised by the experience and the performance of its communist rival. Strong states can also experience political-security threats from integration projects that threaten their state's sovereignty (and their recognition and status). This is clearly illustrated by the political discourse within some EU member states.[145]

Regimes that lack legitimacy are likely to be more vulnerable to threats to political security. Ideas of democracy and revolution may, for example, be invoked as challenges to political security. The Tulip Revolution in Kyrgyzstan (March 2005), the Orange Revolution in Ukraine (late November 2004 to January 2005), and the Rose Revolution in Georgia (November 2003) may be cited as examples of this. The extent to which such "color revolutions" threaten the political security of the respective states has provoked internal state responses that seek to limit the impact of democracy-promotion efforts in their countries.[146]

Another "new" threat to traditional notions of state sovereignty and, thus, to political security stems from the privatization of the use of force. As indicated, a crucial source of state sovereignty originates from its monopoly on the use of force. A growing body of scholarship is documenting the so-called privatization of security. For the first time since the emergence of the nation-state, more military weapons are in the hands of private citizens than in the hands of national governments.[147] While national armies have shrunk by some 20 percent, private groups providing security now outnumber national armies. While the majority of large weapons systems are still held by states, they possess a minority of small arms, which are generally used in low-intensity conflicts.

While mercenary armies, hired by individuals, groups, and ruling regimes, are not new, the private security providers proliferating today are more sophisticated, better organized, and frequently officially registered and sanctioned by governments. They also operate in line with a corporate model that makes them only minimally different from other types of companies. A private security group can also pay its employees more than many national governments can afford.

In addition to internationally active private security groups, indigenous, legitimate security firms and civil defense forces, as well as vigilantes and paramilitary and militia groups, are active within their own countries. These groups operate with varying degrees of acceptance. In some cases, the populace may accept whichever security provider can ensure their safety. In other cases, parts of the population may feel that their security is, in fact, compromised by their presence. In Latin America and the Balkans, some states have outsourced police functions to unscrupulous indigenous paramilitary groups. Some emerge with the objective of maintaining the status quo; others, such as insurgent factions, emerge with the desire to alter the status quo.[148]

Demographic shifts can have a number of implications for political security. In developing states with high fertility rates, a high level of structural unemployment can, according to Brian Nichiporuk, affect domestic politics through the growth in popularity of political groups with radical, revolutionary agendas. In countries where a substantial proportion of the population is between 18 and 24 years old, high levels of youth unemployment, causing considerable frustration, can lead young people to support radical political alternatives to existing regimes. If the leaders of such radical movements succeed in mobilizing a majority of the youth population, this could lead to a full-scale revolution. The existence of large numbers of young people and high levels of youth unemployment in 18th century France is likely to have played a role in the French Revolution. A present-day example of this can be witnessed in Algeria. With a rapidly growing population, the combination of large numbers of young people, high levels of structural unemployment, and the existence of radical Islamic groups has contributed to civil war in the country.

High fertility rates in states that lack the policies and institutions required to fulfill the basic needs of the population may lead to political instability and the complete collapse of government. Explosive population growth may place considerable strain on an already inadequate state infrastructure, as well as exhaust arable land. When these states comprise ethnically mixed patterns of population settlements, a reduction of government control and a history of existing interethnic tensions can spark conflict.[149] Nichiporuk suggests that: "This kind of demographic impact may have been one of the secondary causes of the ethnic strife that has plagued the former Yugoslavia during the last decade. Although Serb hypernationalism and the accompanying quest for a 'Greater Serbia' on the part of Bosnian Serb leader Radovan Karadzic and Serbian President Slobodan Milosevic was the principal cause of the conflicts in Bosnia and Kosovo, the dynamics of differential population growth rates could well have served to fuel Serb feelings of insecurity that had been initially created by these demagogic leaders."[150]

(c) Economic
Another important aspect of national security is economic security, which is related not only to the ensuring the well-being of the population within a state, but also to a state's legitimacy. As the above discussion indicates, economic and political security are interrelated, though their interconnections with other dimensions of security go far beyond this. The idea of economic security is increasingly politicized and controversial. Within the context of economic globalization, economic security is largely shaped by the dominance of the liberal agenda and by the consequences of efforts to implement it in the areas of trade, production, and finance.[151]

In some instances, economic security may be advanced proactively. For example, Singapore maintains a very proactive foreign economic policy. Christopher Dent suggests that this is viewed as an effort to enhance the city-state's economic security. The Singaporean government is very proactive in promoting the country's limited, but high-quality bureaucratic resources to cultivate its economic diplomacy at all levels in order to bring about change that serves its economic advantage. Singapore is frequently described as a global city-state – a post-modern incarnation of the ancient Greek or medieval Italian city-states. It has emerged as a trading center and regional hub that maintains relatively high levels of commercial innovation and economic liberalization. It is, however, highly dependent on foreign direct investment on the part of multinational enterprises for both capital and technology.[152]

Relative wealth is not usually zero-sum in character. As Buzan, Waever, and de Wilde note, the rise of Japan has not made the rest of the Organisation for Economic Co-operation and Development (OECD) poorer. If the Japanese economy were to collapse tomorrow, the resultant loss of capital and markets would drag many other OECD economies down with it.[153] Nevertheless, economic development and the processes of globalization are uneven: While the integration of economic processes is aimed at increasing productivity and growth, the liberalization of commercial and financial markets has brought with it confrontations between states.

If Singapore's foreign economic policy aimed at promoting the city-state as a pole within the global economy represents one expression of the pursuit of economic security in a globalizing economy, more protectionist responses represent another. The phenomenal rise of the Japanese economy in the 1980s, for example, provoked protectionist reactions from the US. The backdrop to this particular trade dispute was the economic recovery and rising competitiveness of both Japan and Europe on the one hand and eroding US competitiveness during the 1970s and 1980s on the other. The US, nevertheless, managed to retain its position by virtue of the shift from the Bretton Woods system to a *de facto* pure dollar system,[154] which effectively allows it to continue to maintain a balance-of-payments deficit. Nevertheless, the economic rise of countries such as China, India, and Brazil may become an increasing source of economic pressure for the US, as well as for other OECD countries, and the temptation to resort to increased protectionism may be strong. The EU's insistence on quotas for Chinese textile imports is indicative of the kinds of pressure already being felt in Europe.

A number of specific issues have been cast in terms of economic security. Many governments argue, for example, that certain strategic industries should be protected. The ability of states to maintain an independent capability for military production in a global market is often viewed as an important dimension of economic security by individual states and, to some extent, by the EU. The supply of energy, particularly oil, is also often considered an issue of economic security. Many fear that economic dependencies on oil will be exploited for political ends.[155] Where the capacity of a state to provide for the well-being of its populace is called into question, the national economy may legitimately be securitized. Yet, it is important to note that a state's failure to meet the needs of its citizens is often a result of poor management of scarce resources.

(d) Societal
National security has been the primary focus of security policy, as well as of academic discussions regarding security. But considerably less attention has been given to exactly what the "national" means in national security. Due to the organizing principle of sovereignty, as explained earlier, the focus of national security has typically been primarily on the political and institutional (including the military) facets of the "nation-state." There has been comparatively less reflection about the nation as a security unit. Societal security is closely related to, and interrelated with, political security.[156]

Societal security, as it is being used here, should not be confused with the Copenhagen School's use of the term, which focuses on identity. Understood in this way, societal security refers to conditions under which communities perceive their identity to be threatened.[157] There are likely to be several communities within any one state. And, as Ole Waever has noted, the level of security experienced by a society as a whole, understood as the entire population of a state, will probably differ from that experienced by various constituent communities within that society.[158] Here, the societal dimension of national security is concerned with the protection of the state population, a group that may not always carry a common identity. Understood in this way, German society is the population within the German state, which contains many other smaller units (German, Arab, Turk, Slav, etc.). It does not imply identification among these people on the basis of language, blood, or culture.

A number of issues may dominate societal security as we define it, such as migration, the disparity between rich and poor, social movements, demographic decline, and health. Many threats to societal security are intimately related to political security, due to their pertinence for the legitimacy of institutionalized order. Societal security implies ensuring, for example, that political power is employed in the service of society as a whole and not just that of a government or regime. It also involves being able to police the entire territory of a state, which is also relevant to political security. Societal and human security are also, of course, closely related, since both types of security concerns include issues that are linked to individual well-being. While there is a clear overlap of issues, specific implications arise from them in relation to the security of society as a whole that may differ from those for individual or human security.

A major challenge facing modern state structures is the current influx of legal and illegal migration for economic, political, and social reasons. While people have migrated throughout history, we are now witnessing an intensification of migratory flows. There are an estimated 191 million migrants globally (2005), which marginally exceeds previous figures (176 million in 2000).[159]

Against this backdrop, one of the state's major security challenges is to ensure that migrant groups coexist with more established groups in society in a way that is not detrimental to society as a whole. Indeed, the interaction between migrants and host societies is part of a comprehensive immigration policy. The societal-security challenge for states in this instance is in how to welcome and employ this new element of the labor force and members of society while also maintaining border control and managing the influx of people.[160] This is an imperative today, given that the question is not one of whether to have migration, but of how to manage it effectively.

Another challenge to the security of society as a whole is the growing disparity between rich and poor. Within the context of a globalizing economy, resources may be unevenly distributed. Some geographic areas within states may be less able to support and maintain large numbers of people than others. While globalization can facilitate economic development, which can help to reduce disparities in wealth, uneven globalization can create divisions within communities and within society as a whole. Within such a context, people and regions may be at risk of marginalization. Unless dealt with effectively, this may generate social tensions and conflicts. National security, therefore, comprises an important societal dimension. As Bethany Webster notes, the challenge for states is to find a balance between desired prosperity at the state level and prosperity at the individual and societal level.[161]

Demographic decline is a current societal-security issue that is receiving increasing attention within both policy and academic circles. While demographic issues have constituted a constant concern throughout the modern era, a number of present-day trends are heightening the importance of issues of demography for national-security policy makers. On the one hand, the end of the Cold War has permitted a widening of the scope of Security Studies, as discussed earlier. On the other hand, the intensification of global communications in recent years has also brought the nexus between demographic change and global instability in far-flung regions to the attention of policy makers worldwide.[162]

Low population growth rates have a number of national-security implications. First, shrinking numbers of youth in some countries will mean that fewer young people will be available for military service. In many countries, this may not pose a security threat in itself, if military technology can compensate for this. A shift from manpower to capital-intensive military forces may, however, increase the fiscal burden of defense for such countries.[163] This may also have more positive spin-offs, however, such as increased multilateral cooperation in the military domain. The EU's European Security and Defence Policy is in part driven by the inability and reticence of individual states to fund the development of capital-intensive military forces individually. The only way that they can afford to develop a credible crisis-management force that is capable of participating in more militarily robust operations is to cooperate in the area of research and development, as well as that of procurement. Second, aging populations will increasingly overstretch welfare states. The EU, for instance, is attempting to implement policies aimed at countering the demographic decline.[164] It is essential for may countries to receive young, inexpensive workers from other countries to fill the jobs that their own populations are unwilling to fill in order to help fund pensions, for example.

States in Africa, Asia, and the Middle East that are experiencing high population growth rates face a different set of security issues.

Growth rates in the Middle East, for example, are putting pressure on the water supplies of many countries in the region. In Central Asia as well, states with high population growth rates surrounding the Aral Basin are already experiencing freshwater shortages as a consequence of irrigation demands, on the one hand, and contamination caused by the use of agrochemicals, on the other. Tensions between states facing high population growth rates may be aggravated by high rates of population growth in any given state, due to migration flows, resource competition, or even shifts in military balances, for example.

The stress on natural resources caused by demographic changes can combine with the socioeconomic stratification of society within developing countries to produce a resource distribution that reflects the existing balance between social classes. As a consequence, members of lower socioeconomic classes may be forced to divide already meager plots of land among themselves as the population grows. This, in turn, can result in a reduction in the availability of land per capita, as well as environmental damage. Overuse of the land will eventually result in lower crop yields and a downward cycle of productivity and living standards. In post-World War II Philippines, for example, population increases intertwined with a property-ownership regime that allocated most the country's fertile land to a small number of wealthy landowners. This caused already-small family plots of land to be further divided as new generations came of age. In time, increasing numbers of Filipino peasants were compelled to move to less fertile land, which was rapidly depleted, causing anger and resentment among the peasants and the growth of insurgent groups in the 1980s.[165]

As pointed out earlier, health issues have long been central to determining our fate and human security,[166] though health has traditionally not been considered a security concern. Nevertheless, recent potential health threats, particularly within the context of increased transnationalization of food production, travel, and migration, force us to think of health as a paramount security concern. At the state level, health is central to the well-being of society as a whole. The capacity to respond effectively to health issues depends on the existence of an adequately functioning and widely accessible healthcare system, as well as on well-managed scarce resources.

(e) Achievement and Challenges
In the military realm, the major challenge that many states face today in the global North is adjusting their armed forces to perform the tasks demanded of them by a security environment that is considerably different from that of the Cold War. In the Euro-Atlantic area, this has been the primary driver behind changes in force structures and strategy in recent years. Force structures within states have traditionally been oriented toward defense of national territory. Yet, the end of the Cold War, increasing willingness to intervene in intrastate conflicts, and the growth of transnational threats has meant that states require both civil and military capabilities that can be deployed for a wide range of tasks, even in far-flung areas of the world, in order to respond to more widely defined challenges to security. While much progress has been made, it is clear that this still poses a challenge.

Challenges in the area of political security are highly contentious issues to deal with. This is because security arguments may be used by governments that lack legitimacy and wish to use repressive means to maintain their position of government. While democratic governments represent the people, this is not always the case, particularly where certain groups are not adequately involved in the political process, as was the case before the advent of women's suffrage and the civil-rights movements.[167] The challenge is to stabilize institutionalized authority in a way that serves the interests of the respective population. States that have already achieved the organizational stability of their social orders are likely to feel less threatened by challenges to their legitimacy.

The organizing concept of political security is sovereignty. As explained, a crucial basis of state sovereignty is a monopoly on the use of force. In general, private security groups are not perceived as a threat to states. However, in states that have a non-existent or precarious monopoly on the use of armed force, they pose a greater problem. For states that actively and openly outsource military and police-related activities to private security groups, the challenge is to ensure that these groups act ethically within the framework of regulation.

States also face the challenge of ensuring the economic well-being of their populations. A state's failure to meet this challenge is often a result of poor management of scarce resources. Within the context of globalization, given the associated dominance of the liberal agenda, many states may find it hard to maintain current levels of economic prosperity. An important dimension in achieving this will be the recognition that relative wealth is not a zero-sum game. States have a common interest in developing multilateral arrangements and institutions that are better able to regulate and deal with commercial and financial instabilities that accompany liberalization of these markets.

In relation to societal security, the implications of demographic changes are only beginning to be recognized as security concerns. Dealing with demographic change partly involves finding ways to welcome young immigrant forces who can both contribute to economic growth and help to support overstretched welfare systems in many countries. It also involves policies that encourage maternity. In the great majority of states, however, women often have to choose between having children and pursuing a career. States also face the challenge of reintegrating women who have taken career breaks into the workplace.

5. Transnational Security

The fourth substrate of global security is transnational security, which involves the globalization-mediated security of states against transnational threats that refer to any type of illegal cross-border movements. Transnational threats include, *inter alia*, terrorism, organized crime, human and drug trafficking, cyber-crime, and the traffic of weapons. There are also other transnational challenges such as irregular migration and environmental degradation. The implications of current threats are far-reaching and multifaceted. Thus, responses to such threats must be similar in scope, applicability, and complexity.

(a) The Concept of Transnational Security
Until fairly recently, the source of threats to security were assumed to primarily emanate from other states and to be military in nature. With the end of the Cold War, however, a number of "new" threats to security gained prominence on the security agenda. These included weapons proliferation, drug trafficking, and international organized crime, among others. These phenomena were for the most part transnational in nature.

Transnational may be defined as "extending or going beyond national borders."[168] Contemporary security threats are often transnational in that they are rarely confined to Westphalian state actors. Specifically, transnational security threats refer to security challenges that transcend international borders and threaten the political, social, or economic integrity of a nation or the quality of life or livelihood of its inhabitants. They generally affect a particular nation or its inhabitants either because of their inherent characteristics, e.g., air or water pollution that spreads across boundaries due to water currents or prevailing winds, or as the result of inadequate management of related issues by governments. In the latter case, this may be the result of either a lack of institutional and governance capacities or a lack of willingness to deal with a particular problem.

Transnational threats are also challenging because they emerge over indefinite, often long periods of time, which means that they may not receive adequate attention from governments, which are primarily concerned with short-term problems, largely due to concerns about being re-elected. The principal actors driving many transnational threats are also non-state actors, such as criminal and terrorist networks, and traffickers of various kinds. This poses considerable problems for states and many state-based arrangements that have been established to deal with security issues, since non-state actors are generally not concerned with treaty making or international law. In fact, non-state actors tend to elude state institutions and governments rather than enter into negotiations with them.

As Paul J. Smith notes in his article "Transnational Security Threats and State Survival: A Role for the Military?" the growth of transnational organized crime has become identified as a prime security concern in the post-Cold War period. A global context that enables the easy movement of capital, people, and goods also creates increased opportunities for individuals and groups to engage in illegal activities, including the trafficking of arms, drugs, and human beings, as well as money laundering. Transnational crime presents a long-drawn-out threat to states. Linkages between organized criminal structures and state institutions can undermine states with emerging democratic institutions. Many countries in Eastern Europe and the Caucasus are in the midst of extremely difficult transitions from state socialism to free-market democracies, and are now experiencing corruption and organized crime on a large scale. Clan- or family-based criminal groups have in many instances transformed into transnational criminal networks.[169] These groups are particularly difficult to deal with because of their success in penetrating societal structures.[170]

(i) Organized Crime
The growth of organized crime is a transnational threat that is in part made possible by corrupt law-enforcement officers and officials. This makes it hard even for well-meaning governments to tackle the problem. The collapse of state authority structures following the fall of communist regimes, in many instances, left a power vacuum that was filled by criminal organizations. Criminal organizations have been able to make significant inroads into society and state institutional structures.[171]

(ii) International Terrorism
While international terrorism has existed since the 1970s in the form of so-called Euro-terrorism, it has rocketed to the top of the security agendas of states since the attacks in Washington and New York in 2001, in Madrid in 2004, and in London in 2005. While terrorist attacks have not necessarily increased, their destructiveness has raised the stakes for governments and state security forces. Like organized criminal groups, terrorist networks have benefited from the communications revolution and advanced financial services. Changes in the international system have also precipitated the emergence and consolidation of terrorist groups motivated by religious extremism. The black market for arms provides many terrorist groups with weapons. Porous borders and migration also play a role in facilitating international terrorism.

Terrorism can impact states in a number of ways, either through casualties and fatalities, or by targeting infrastructure which is critical to daily activity such as information systems and communications. Additionally, it may put pressure on a state to react in a way which can potentially infringe on civil liberties.

(iii) International Migration
International migration has also become a central security concern for states. As a result of the current scale at which people are able to move around the world, immigration and asylum seekers sometimes become identified as national security issues. The alarming manner in which states are reacting to this seems to be, at least in part, related to the ambiguity surrounding the social, economic, and cultural implications of immigration. Terrorist attacks in New York, Washington, Madrid and London over the past few years have also added to concerns about international migration and immigration.[172]

While there is a need for imported skilled and unskilled labor in many countries, particularly against the backdrop changing demographic trends, uncontrolled migration may pose problems for host countries.[173] Unsolicited migration risks generating nationalistic and xenophobic responses within receiving countries, as more established communities perceive, with or without reason, that their jobs and wages are at risk.[174] The problem exists for both source countries as they lose their skilled workers and those that receive the labor as these potential responses are generated. The societal security implications for both the receiving and source country may, therefore, be significant.

(iv) Human Trafficking
Many people are willing to put themselves at great risk to attempt to enter other countries illegally; as a result, they are extremely vulnerable to human trafficking. The smuggling and trafficking of human beings has become a worldwide "industry," with a turnover of billions of dollars a year.[175] In June 2000, British Customs authorities discovered the bodies of 58 would-be Chinese illegal immigrants in a truck at Dover. This incident helped to highlight the danger posed to individuals by illicit means of entering a country.[176] Spain's Canary Islands have become a gateway to Europe for many migrants from Africa. A Chinese criminal network is known to have been involved in the recent trafficking of people from Guinea to the Canary Islands.[177]

Moreover, those who survive often dangerous journeys may be subjected to hazardous working conditions and abuse on arrival, due to their lack of legal status. A recent case of a forced-work camp in southern Italy illustrates this point. Having initially come from Poland in order to engage in seasonal work in the Italian agricultural sector, workers received half the legal wage and were obliged to reimburse the cost of transportation to the farms, in addition to their room and board. This placed them in an indebted and very vulnerable situation.[178] Transnational challenges such as these are clearly interlinked with human security concerns.

(v) Health
Many governments have come to view the spread of infectious diseases not simply as a public health concern but as a threat to security. Infectious diseases are age-old threats to people's well-being and livelihood. The plague, or Black Death, of the 14th century resulted in

more fatalities over a five-year period than that of any military conflict before or since.[179] Over the last thirty years, the world has witnessed the emergence of new infectious diseases, such as AIDS. In December 1998, there were more than 33.4 million people around the world living with HIV (the virus that causes AIDS) or fully developed AIDS. It has been estimated that the number of people with HIV had grown to more than 100 million by 2005. Africa remains the most severely affected region, with around 10,000 new infections a day.[180] However, many other areas of the world are suffering the debilitating effects of the disease, including parts of Asia. It is now believed that India has the highest number of people infected with HIV.

The resurgence of old diseases has accompanied recent, new diseases. This is occurring for a number of reasons, however, can partly be linked to urban crowding, migration, overuse of antibiotics, and poor public healthcare systems. Tuberculosis is once such disease. In Africa, more than 1.6 million new cases of tuberculosis occur each year, which results in approximately 600,000 deaths. In China, it is the country's most lethal infectious disease.[181]

(vi) Environmental Degradation
Environmental degradation is still a major transnational security challenge. Environmental security encompasses a gamut of challenges, such as global climate change, water and air pollution, and degradation of scarce resources. Poor governance and weak institutions are often at the heart of environmental insecurity. At one level, environmental crises are not just linked to environmental degradation and scarcity of resources, but also to the lack of, or the inadequate nature of, environmental-management policies. Lack of institutional or governance capacities can often help to account for human insecurity resulting from a lack of scarce resources or the degradation of environmental resources.[182]

As Frank McNeil notes, environmental damage can lead to the increased severity of natural disasters, wreak severe economic harm, cause societal instability, and even contribute to conflicts within nations, as well as across borders.[183] Global climate change is arguably the most serious long-term environmental threat. Rising sea levels, a result of climate change, will become a growing challenge for coastal regions around the world. Indeed, many Asian countries consider global climate change as their major security concern.[184] Transboundary pollution in some regions of the world is so serious that it has generated tensions between neighboring states. Disputes over transboundary water management,[185] such as between Mexico and the United States, as well as in the Nile Basin, the Jordan Basin, and the Ganges Basin,[186] are all notable examples of conflicts between states over water-related issues.

Global social, economic, and political changes that have occurred over the last two decades have contributed to the existence and severity of these phenomena. The collapse of communism has plunged many societies and states into difficult political and economic transitions that have placed a strain on many former communist states that still have relatively weak state institutions and governance capacities. Institutionalized human-smuggling routes, for example, are made possible because of weak legislation, inadequate border controls, corrupt officials, as well as the influence of organized crime.[187] Elsewhere in the world, particularly in sub-Saharan Africa, failed states are contributing to many contemporary transnational threats, such as HIV/AIDS and illegal migration. The people of many of these countries are also vulnerable to human traffickers as they seek opportunities outside their countries of origin. Large parts of the territories of failing or failed states may be outside the control of state authorities, making it prime terrain for criminal or terrorist activities.

(b) Achievements and Challenges
Traditionally, state and non-state security services have been the principal actors that have taken on the task of protecting populations. The military played a role in maintaining peace and stability in a number of regions prior to and during the Cold War, and it continues to do so today. Military involvement in responses to transnational threats suggests a transformation of the role of the military. It is increasingly involved, for example, in policing state borders, alongside border-security agencies. This is particularly notable in the case of the EU, for example. In some instances, involvement of the military may be necessary and it may be prudent for states to prepare their armed forces to deal with some transnational threats. It may not, however, always be appropriate. Military interventions may even protract conflicts and human suffering across borders, leading to war economies and the growth of organized criminal networks.

In the face of many current transnational realities, including migration and irregular immigration, xenophobic and exclusionary tendencies in host societies with regard to race, political beliefs, and religion are being generated. Increased awareness of diversity might help to reduce the severity of this dimension of the problem. In the case of international terrorism, most experts agree that a better cultural understanding and historical knowledge would help to prevent the root causes of terrorism, notably humiliation. Indeed, this would be useful at any level of application in current state decision-making systems.

Regional and international institutions have played an important role in establishing and maintaining peace and security throughout the international system. Institutions such as the North Atlantic Treaty Organisation, the European Union, the United Nations, the African Union, and the League of Arab States have all been tasked with dealing with issues of peace and security. They are often successful in implementing short-term solutions to some security challenges, yet the root causes are all too often not addressed.

Transnational threats to security also call into question the efficacy of state-based regimes. For instance, in the case of non-proliferation, the growth of non-state proliferators poses a challenge to the nuclear non-proliferation regime, which is designed to deal with proliferation by states. Similarly, transnational health issues require a transnational approach. Despite this, health has tended to be considered a state matter. What these examples illustrate is that state-centered paradigms need to be reformulated if states are to be successful in meeting the multitude of security challenges they face.

One of the challenges facing regional and international security management is the difficulty of establishing common norms among participating states, which is vital if states are, for instance, required to respond rapidly to crises. In addition, the success of joint policy endeavors and missions will depend on the capabilities available. Crisis-management capabilities, for instance, must be multifaceted and perhaps capable of deployment in distant parts of the world. Cooperation in areas that are central to traditional conceptions of state sovereignty, such as defense, law enforcement, and intelligence, while essential, is likely to meet considerable resistance.

6. Transcultural Security

The fifth substrate of security that we propose is transcultural security, which refers not to the security of state populations, but to the integrity of diverse cultures and civilizational forms. Culture has usually been marginalized by the traditional security paradigm informed by realism. The Copenhagen School's sectoral approach to security went a long way to defining cultural issues as security concerns. Being conscious of the security of groups and cultures within states is especially pertinent within the context of transnational realities linked to migration and irregular immigration and xenophobic and exclusionary tendencies in host societies with regard to culture, political beliefs, and religion.

In our view, the idea of competing cultures needs to be expanded. There needs not only to be a *modus vivendi*, but a synergy found between cultures and civilizations. At the transnational level, alliance building and the coexistence of civilizations will be crucial to dealing effectively with transnational threats to security. This is particularly the case in an age of intensified transcultural interaction. However, the notion of synergy implies much more. It holds that a plurality of cultures can have a net effect on global security that is greater than would be the case if representatives of individual cultures acted individually. Transcultural security is nevertheless a vital component of achieving the objective of transcultural synergy.

(a) The Concept of Transcultural Security

Security Studies and much of security-policy thinking have tended to neglect the importance of culture in determining security at various levels. The Copenhagen School's sectoral approach to security made a great contribution to bringing cultural questions into view. Indeed, according to Peter Hough, "Undoubtedly, the most influential idea to emerge from the conceptual widening of Security Studies in the 1990s by the Copenhagen School was that of societal security."[188] This concept suggests that security issues go beyond threats to states or their populations and include particular kinds of societies.[189]

Societal security, as Buzan, Waever, and de Wilde define it, takes its cue from the observation that collective identities exist that are not necessarily coterminous with those of the state. The societal sector, according to their understanding of it, is comprised of large-scale collective identities that are capable of functioning independently from the state. Tribes, clans, nations, nation-like ethnic units or minorities, civilizations, and religions may constitute such collectivities.[190]

Communities are formed by individuals who identify with each other because, for example, of a common history, language, religion, political ideology, or geographic location. In security terms, the ideas and practices that help to constitute a collective identity are of primary concern. Thus, identity is the organizing concept within the societal-security sector, as defined by the Copenhagen School.

Threats to identity always involve the construction of some "we" feeling. A "we" or common identity can be constructed in a number of ways. Whether issues become security concerns depends on which self-definition wins out in a community. Some of the most common issues that are invoked as threats to societal security are migration, competition with a neighboring or dominant culture, and depopulation. But whether migrants or rival identities are securitized depends on whether the holders of a collective identity take a closed-minded or open-minded view of how their identity is constituted and maintained.[191]

Despite his praise for the contribution of the Copenhagen School, Hough argues that defining cultural change as a security matter risks diluting the concept of security too much. Nevertheless, he does concede that: "In spite of these reservations about societal security, the Copenhagen School did a service to International Relations in further releasing the discipline from its state-centric straightjacket. Surely one of the clearest limitations of the traditional notion of 'national security' (where the referent is the state) comes from the fact that it excludes from consideration the political killing of people by their own government or other sections of society. Individuals die because of social constructions, however abstract and subjective they may be."[192]

In our view, questions of identity and cultural change are important security issues that deserve more attention than they currently receive. Within the current context marked by intense human mobility and instantaneous connectivity, being conscious of the security of groups and cultures within states is especially important if we wish to reduce xenophobic and exclusionary tendencies in host societies with regard to race, political beliefs, and religion. Ultimately, we need to seek not only coexistence between cultural groups and civilizations, but a synergy between them. This belief is based upon the notion that a plurality of cultures can have a net impact on global security that exceeds that of individual cultures.

(b) Threats to Transcultural Security
At the state level, problems are arising where diverse communities are not positively integrated into a larger societal structure that is often

constructed as a homogeneous entity. Given intensified migration, facilitated in part by improvements in travel, communications, and uneven development, many states comprise a number of communities with different cultural heritages. Today, many societies are extremely diverse and include individuals with a profusion of identifying characteristics, making it potentially harder for states to integrate them into an existing, overarching culture. Where the state has failed to promote diversity and tolerance within its state and social structures, these often competing cultures can be a source of tension and conflict. This may be most likely to occur in instances where disjunctures exist between people's cultural heritage and that of the more established community, either through exclusive language policies and legislation or in more subtle forms of discrimination. In such a situation, large sections of a state's population are likely to become marginalized, which may, in turn, lead to feelings of injustice and frustration.[193]

Feelings of shame, fear, and rage are inextricably linked to perceptions of injustice and alienation. People in despair tend to harbor a fatalistic attitude toward their own existence, which results from a belief that they have no influence over a negative life situation and, consequently, have no future. This may lead to tension and conflict between diverse communities within a state population. The problem is likely to be particularly acute in countries that have large immigrant communities. As Webster notes: "Quite often, people are connected by culture, traditions, customs, language, or religion rather than the nation-state in which they live. This was also the case during the time of the Reformation (and directly after), when a person's place in society was determined by religion rather than state citizenship (Ireland provides a good example)."[194] Western European states are prime examples of this. Much will be determined by the place in society a particular national identity affords other minorities. Thus, states face the challenge of promoting a national identity that is capable of accommodating all cultures within society as a whole.

The notion of culture as a source of insecurity has been evoked in the recent past within academic literature, most notably by Samuel Huntington in his book *The Clash of Civilizations*. Huntington depicts cultures or cultural regions, i.e., "civilizations," as independen social entities and major actors in international relations. Yet, cultures are treated by Huntington as rigid structures.[195] Confucianism, Buddhism, Hinduism, Islam, and Western culture are treated as if they were clearly definable, monolithic, homogeneous entities. This overlooks the variations and contradictions within these civilizations, some of which have generated, and still do generate, internal fissures. Robert Lieber and Ruth Weisberg support this point in their article "Globalization, Culture, and Identities in Crisis." They stress that "the ultimate clash is less between civilizations than *within* them."[196]

As Dieter Senghaas points out, an international cultural debate cannot be productive if cast in these terms. It is important to be aware that culture may be elevated to a security issues when the members of large collective identities feel under threat as the result of change. According to Senghaas, the process by which cultural groups differentiate themselves from others has traditionally formed an essential part of their development. Conflicts within cultures over fundamental principles have also been part of their evolution. Yet, in a world of instant connectivity linked to the rapidity with which information can be exchanged and human mobility, this process of transformation may result in cultural turmoil.

A good place for transcultural dialogue to start, as Senghaas argues, is the differentiation processes that are now taking place within traditional cultures. It is particularly important to pay attention to the confusion that changes in the global environment may be generating. In culturally pluralistic societies, such disarray may undermine political security by calling into question the legitimacy of the state. As a result, one of the major security challenges facing states today is the need find a way of including all of the cultural groups that comprise society.[197]

Conflicts that are generated as a result of culture are unfolding where societies are undergoing rapid and sometimes intense change. However, present-day transformations are different from those that occurred in Europe in the past.[198] Today, change and conflicts over fundamental principles within cultures are taking place within a global environment largely defined by American hegemony. In relation to Islam, there is a tendency in the West to focus on extremism. Yet, there is a spectrum of views within Islam. In order to deal with extremism, it will be important to address its root causes and to marginalize its appeal. This implies gaining greater awareness of the range of views within the Muslim world as to how to deal with the far-reaching changes it is undergoing. Indigenous solutions to social ills and grievances that are more appropriate for the societies concerned are likely to be more successful than external models that reflect the historical and cultural development of other regions. As Senghaas proposes,

"An appraisal of forward-looking thinking in the Islamic world (and elsewhere) – first by simply acknowledging its existence, making translations and organizing dialogues – is much more promising for the future than a continuation of distorted debates on fundamentalism."[199]

(c) Achievements and Challenges

The challenge facing many developed states across the world is how to promote a national identity that is premised on the promotion of diversity and respect of differences. This is a particularly pressing issue for states that are increasingly dependent upon immigration to sustain current levels of growth, as well as to maintain functioning welfare states. Against the backdrop of tensions within society, due to poorly integrated, less established communities, some states have responded with policy initiatives designed to dissuade members of certain groups from either immigrating to, or seeking citizenship within, their countries.

Some states and societies appear to be responding by making it more of a challenge for particular communities and groups to integrate in societies. When states follow policies that marginalize certain groups of people within their borders, it can alienate people and cause feelings of frustration and anger. Additionally, it may be misinterpreted and create unnecessary difficulties for those who are trying to integrate. In order to avoid this, states must promote diversity and tolerance in all aspects. This implies facilitating increased awareness about "the other" and empowering communities that are underrepresented to encourage both their inclusion in society and to create greater opportunities for their integration.

One of the more pressing security issues of the modern era is linked to how countries manage cultural pluralism and advance the ideals of transcultural security. Globalization can create tension both within and between cultures as a result of increased contact with distant "others" and the introduction of new ideas and technologies. Adaptation of non-Western societies with different civilizational heritages to a Western-, and especially US-, dominated global system may, therefore, be the source of friction.

Evaluating current policy decisions that are aimed at dealing with transcultural issues that potentially conflict with a state culture and identity, such as the printing of the Mohammed cartoons in Denmark, can be understood more cohesively if we employ the lens of transcultural security.[200]

We need to find ways of spreading knowledge that might serve to nurture co-existence among people and groups in a globalizing world. Reducing ignorance about one another is vital if we are to live together in harmony. Thus, combating ignorance in all its forms is a crucial consideration for all states. Human beings must respect one another in all their diversity of belief, culture, and language. Differences between and within societies should not be feared or repressed. In fact, cross-fertilization should be understood as a strength rather than something to fear. Peaceful coexistence between civilizations depends upon mutual recognition and respect. Indeed, our capacity for self-development will be determined by our ability to learn from others.[201] As Hans Koechler notes: "The self-comprehension of a civilization and the appreciation of its values have to be embedded in an inter-civilizational framework of mutual exchange. Civilizations that aspire to be present in the global framework today have to accept the fact of interdependence."[202] We must encourage transcultural synergy if we wish to find long-term solutions to many of the security challenges we face today.

7. Conclusion

In this chapter, we outlined a new classification of global security in an effort to offer a more comprehensive vision and approach to global security. In our view, global security should be thought of analytically as consisting of five dimensions of security. The five dimensions, or substrates, of global security comprised within the pentagon were identified as **human, environmental, national, transnational, and transcultural** security. Our aim in classifying global security in this way is to provide a framework that is capable of identifying the diverse array of phenomena that impact individual, state, and cultural security. In particular, this classification aims to bring the issue of transcultural relations, traditionally marginalized by realism, to center stage.

We discussed each of the substrates of global security individually within each section of the chapter. The first substrate, human security, refers to the security of individuals. The second, environmental security, refers to the security of the biosphere. The third substrate, national security, refers to the state's population, economic situation, and organizational integrity. The fourth is transnational security, which refers to the security of states against illegal transboundary issues. The fifth is transcultural security, which refers to ensuring that a plurality of cultures and civilizations can coexist without their relations being elevated to security issues. We then discussed some of the most prevalent issues within each security domain, as well as briefly reviewed achievements and remaining challenges.

We pointed out that while global security may analytically be divided into our five suggested substrata, these dimensions are in reality interrelated. Alleviating human insecurity may, for example, require ameliorating environmental security, national security, transnational security, and transcultural security, or some combination of these. For instance, ill-health as a result of water pollution may also represent a transnational security challenge in that it affects a lake surrounded by a number of countries and require cooperation between several national authorities. Another example of interconnections may be human rights abuses affecting human, societal, and transcultural security.

CHAPTER 4

JUSTICE AS A PREREQUISITE FOR SECURITY

1. Introduction

In the preceding chapter, we proposed a new classification of global security in an effort to provide a more comprehensive approach to global security. Our classification comprised five substrates of security. The five that we identified were **human, environmental, national, transnational, and transcultural security**. As the previous chapter illustrated, these substrates are often interrelated. Nevertheless, separating them analytically is helpful since it allows for a variation of referent objects of security and is useful insofar as it indicates a variety of means with which to advance security.

In our view, one of the main means of enhancing global security is the pursuit of justice, not only within political communities inside states but also within the wider global context. While it may seem self-evident that justice constitutes a fundamental consideration when formulating policies, justice as a fundamental security concern is all too often overlooked by policy makers, who may be inclined to view it as a philosophical rather than national-security question. Yet, many of the security challenges that we face today have as their root cause injustice of one kind or another. Consider, for instance, a multi-ethnic country in which tensions are rising between the ethnic majority and an ethnic minority, who not only suffer from discrimination but also the systematic violation of their basic human rights. Tension is growing between these two communities due to the mobilization of the minority community and its struggle for equal treatment, rendering the situation for individuals, communities, the state, and the region increasingly insecure and unstable. At the heart of this hypothetical security problem is injustice as a result of unequal treatment that violates the dignity of those who do not enjoy full civil and human rights. At the most elementary level, this security concern is fundamentally about justice. Justice, therefore, forms a central dimension of our proposed new security principle, the **multi-sum security principle**.

In this chapter, we focus on the security implications of injustice and the significance of justice for the advancement of global security. Specifically, injustice is important because it generates feelings of humiliation, frustration, and anger. This, in turn, can lead people to experience alienation from the societies and institutions that are supposed to represent them. The use of military force alone in the pursuit of security will not work if there is continued real or perceived injustice anywhere in the world by groups, states, sub-national cultural groups or supranational civilizational forms. This is because people who wish to propagate insecurity and instability will find fertile ground for their warped ideas in places where there is injustice. Indeed, within such contexts, their ideas about how to alleviate injustice are likely to have mass appeal, no matter how illogical, futile, or violent they may be. The only way to marginalize and render these extreme groups ineffective is to remove their appeal to the masses. This means promoting greater justice in the world. While there will always be extreme elements in societies, their attraction will be mitigated if justice is understood as a prerequisite of security and is rigorously pursued. Without justice, long-term security will be out of reach.

First, we begin by briefly outlining the concept of justice. Second, we examine the relationship between injustice, whether real or perceived, and feelings of frustration, anger, and humiliation. Third, we discuss how such sentiments are connected to alienation, which risks degenerating into extreme forms of action, including terrorism and violent conflict. Fourth, we offer some examples that illustrate how real or perceived injustice can lead to feelings of humiliation, alienation, frustration, and anger. Finally, we argue that justice is imperative if lasting security and stability are to be achieved.

2. Injustice and Insecurity

Social psychologists have some valuable insights into the forces that unite or divide people from others, ignite emotions, and contribute to people's readiness to engage in various forms of violence. According to Elaine Hatfield and Richard L. Rapson, people in all cultures are concerned with social justice, kindness, and compassion. While these concepts may be defined differently, concern with them reflects people's belief that one should treat others with kindness and compassion.²⁰³

While the concept of justice is frequently employed, what it means is seldom clear. Justice may be thought of as generally referring to a morally correct distribution of benefits and burdens. What justice is taken to assess, of course, varies, though it is often invoked in relation to political structures and the distribution of goods, as well as behavior and character traits. The precise content of justice is therefore determined by the objects evaluated rather than by the set of moral concerns relevant for the assessment. This means that its meaning will be context-specific. As a concept, justice has a number of potential meanings. First, it may refer to what we morally owe others. Second, it may refer to personal wrongs done to others, based on what they may claim from us. Third, justice may be concerned with enforceable duties. Fourth, justice may refer to meeting the demands of what is owed. A fifth sense of justice may refer to fairness, where this is understood in purely comparative terms.²⁰⁴

While the idea of justice within the state has provided numerous and clear responses to what justice might require within the state, international or global justice has presented moral philosophy with far more intractable dilemmas. For some, justice within the domestic sphere is possible primarily because a type of contractual relationship exists between the state and citizens: The state takes on the task of ensuring that justice is administered and citizens accept that the state has a legitimate role in doing so, as long as it accepts certain limits on its sovereign right. Part of the reason why it is able to administer justice is it's monopoly on the legitimate use of force.

In the international realm, institutional arrangements, though some exist, do not imply the same kind of contractual relationship and no global institution has a legitimate monopoly on the use of force with which to ensure that justice is administered. As a result the requirements of justice are less significant than in the domestic realm. What we currently have reflects a multilayered order of moral commitments.²⁰⁵

Within the field of security, justice has tended to be relegated to the domestic sphere in large part because of the intellectual hegemony of the realist paradigm within the discipline of IR. While not all realists deny the possibility of moral behavior, its application to state behavior in the international realm is not considered feasible or even desirable. States are believed to be above all driven by the need to survive and cannot afford to indulge in the pursuit of the "good life."[206]

Yet, we would argue that the long-term security of a state, cultural group or individual cannot be achieved without taking heed of people's desire for justice. Whatever guise injustice takes, the outcomes in terms of human emotions are likely to include feelings of humiliation, alienation, frustration, and anger. Such feelings are all factors that contribute to tension, which can degenerate into violent conflict and acts of cruelty.

Despite the fairly common-sense relationship between injustice and insecurity, very little contemporary security literature, perhaps with the exception of that dealing with post-conflict security-sector reform, focuses specifically on the issues of injustice and justice. Here, we suggest that it is useful to try to trace the relationship between injustice and insecurity by looking at the interplay of injustice, humiliation, alienation, frustration, and anger. Together these factors can produce extreme forms of behavior that can result in tension and violent behavior.

(a) Injustice and Humiliation
People feel a sense of humiliation when their dignity is violated. This can occur when an abstract ideal about how people in general or citizens in particular should be treated is violated. The abstract ideal that people perceive as being violated is the ideal of respect for the equal dignity of all. Within the domestic context of states, the unequal treatment of one country's citizens may, for example, cause humiliation among those being treated in a way that is inferior to the treatment of others. We might, then, say that feelings of humiliation are created by injustice, understood as what we morally owe others.

Unequal treatment leading to a sense of humiliation may include negative stereotyping or prejudice, both of which rely on socially constructed images of particular groups that serve as lenses that filter information and inform people's behavior. As such, they can be reified or reconstructed, depending on how we interpret the information we receive. Since stereotypes are extremely narrow definitions of people, they are usually based on very little first-hand knowledge of those being depicted. What this means is that negative stereotypes have very little opportunity to be deconstructed and reconstructed in a more positive way. This clearly has serious implications, because negative stereotypes deny the equal worth of those being negatively stereotyped.

Denying the equal worth of people through negative stereotyping can lead to abuse of various kinds, ranging from suspicion, aggression, physical violence, and even genocide. In an environment in which geographic distances have become compressed due to increased travel, innovations in technology, and the increased permeability of national borders, people are confronted with differences in a much more intense way than they once were. As Jan Aart Scholte has noted, "The more that distance and borders have disintegrated, the more national differences have seemed precious."[207] Reactions from more established communities within societies may be predominantly defensive. Thus, in a period of unprecedented migration and increased economic insecurity, relative newcomers to a society and refugees may find themselves exposed to threats to their personal and group security as members of more established communities seek to ward off perceived dangers.

Stereotypes are understood as generalizations of groups of people that claim to capture their inherent features. As such, they render curiosity about the characters and capacities of their individual members unnecessary. As mentioned, negative stereotypes often identify their subjects as being inferior as human beings. Thus, not only is a benefit viewed as irrelevant to a particular individual, but the benefit is considered undeserved. We can observe the linkages between, for example, prejudicial attitudes, negative stereotypes, and opinions regarding welfare recipients. As Peter Burns and James G. Gimpel note in their article on economic insecurity, prejudicial stereotypes, and public opinion on immigration policy: "Blacks and Hispanic are more likely than whites to be the target of negative ethnic stereotypes as the result of attitudes on welfare....[T]hose who think the least of welfare recipients clearly have harsher mental images of blacks and Hispanics than those who are not as critical about the poor."[208] Thus, on the basis of a purely arbitrary judgment, a person's autonomy or power to define significant aspects of his or her life may be reduced.

Prejudice, which we may define as a belief in the inferiority of an individual that leads to a judgment about the unworthiness of that person for a certain benefit, has the same consequence in terms of injustice as negative stereotyping. Yet, prejudicial treatment may also entail intent to do harm to an individual. Thus, while related to negative stereotyping, it is even more dangerous. Rather than simply failing to do justice to an individual's aptitude and circumstances, prejudice goes one step further and involves intent to do harm to a person. It necessarily implies unequal treatment, since it is premised on the assumption that the victims of prejudice are undeserving. For example, government policies that are informed by prejudices are likely to produce or reinforce oppressive power relations. When individuals are oppressed by others, they are denied certain benefits, such as political participation. Prejudice may also lead to practices that deny people their basic needs.[209]

Thus, both prejudice and negative ethnic stereotyping cause feelings of humiliation because they assume that the victims of prejudicial treatment or negative stereotyping are inherently inferior as human beings. Humiliation, in turn, generates feelings of frustration and anger. In order to understand why, we need to incorporate the concept of alienation into our analysis.

(b) Alienation, Anger, and Frustration
The property that appears to be common in various instances of alienation is a sense of a lack of ownership of one's whole self. When we feel alienated, our ownership of our actions is somehow called into question. Karl Marx's notion of alienation implied something similar. Essentially, Marx described workers as alienated from their own activities. What he had in mind was that workers spend most of their time engaged in an activity that is not meaningful to them and the time remaining after work is not spent on things that are meaningful to them either, but on consumption. Marx's notion of alienation also has another dimension. Workers are alienated in the sense that the actions by which they produce goods are not fully their own, since they are compelled to sell their labor. This latter aspect of Marx's concept of alienation finds reverberations in social philosophy.[210]

Writing from a philosophical standpoint, Carol Rovane maintains that there is a common way of considering ownership over one's intentional life and, therefore, about alienation. She explains that, among action theorists within social philosophy, there is a general consensus on a number of points. First, agents have some kind of evaluative commitments with which to evaluate their own actions. Second, they identify with their own actions. Third, they feel alienated by those things within themselves that they do not identify with, i.e., things internal to them that do not fit with their evaluative commitments. For example, certain irritable tendencies may not fit with a person's evaluative commitments. Even though that person may not like such tendencies, he or she, nevertheless, has a relationship of ownership to them.

The sense of ownership that we have, even over things that we disapprove of, presupposes a possibility of betterment. There is thus some distant form of hope of being able to change these things, despite the condition of alienation. It also suggests that people are unhappy with being subjected to a particular form of influence that compels them to act in a way that does not fit with their commitments.

Rovane's discussion of alienation also suggests a possible relationship between injustice, humiliation, anger, and frustration. She points out that there are some circumstances in which other people may lay claim to our actions just as much as we can. In cases of coercion, for example, this is the true source of alienation, since the actions of the person being coerced are literally induced by someone else. This goes some way to understanding how we can feel alienated from our own actions or even our own lives. The choices that we make derive from someone else or even something outside of us. This is, for example, why we assign responsibility for coerced actions to the perpetrators of the coercion.[211]

Taking our cue from Rovane, we may speculate that feelings of frustration, anger, and humiliation originate from carrying out actions or living our lives in ways that do not accord with our evaluative commitments and potential. Being coerced either directly or indirectly is alienating because it separates us from ourselves as whole beings capable of agency in its fullest sense.

Alienation is usually used to refer to estrangement from others. The connection between injustice, humiliation, and alienation may be explained by a separation from one's true self in the sense of being induced to act in a way that one cannot identify with. Essentially, our identities and actions become fractured as a result of the way in which others define or treat us. Being treated as inferior to what we are as human beings and denied full agency not surprisingly leads to feelings of anger and frustration.

Yet, the fact that we recognize our actions or aspects of our lives to induce alienation from our true selves implies, as mentioned, the recognition that change is possible. Therefore, some degree of hope, however faint, may simultaneously exist with feelings of alienation. While people may be experiencing despair in relation to their own lives, they may nevertheless hold out the hope of contributing to changing a broader political context in the future. Anger and frustration borne out of limited agency could, and frequently do, lead to dramatic actions aimed at contributing to a different future.

There are countless examples of contemporary security questions that serve to demonstrate how alienation is central to understanding why real or perceived injustice is likely to lead to insecurity. For example, the conflict between Israel and Palestine provides a prominent example where a longing for justice has gone unsatisfied. Both sides in this ongoing conflict harbor a deep sense of injustice: Jews have a strong sense of injustice because of how they were treated in the past; Palestinians' sense of injustice is generated because of how they are treated now. While we focus on the latter, this is in no way intended to suggest that it is a more important element in explaining the endless cycle of violence that characterizes this conflict.

Similarly, terrorism is often characterized as a force for destabilizing governments, economies, and a major cause of global instability. At one level, all of these things are true. Nevertheless, a number of additional factors have to be borne in mind. First, this understanding of terrorism emerged in the late 18th and early 19th centuries. As such, it reflects the primary referents of security at that time, namely man and the state, and, as a consequence of the latter, the preoccupation with state sovereignty.[212]

3. Justice and Long-term Security

(a) The Futility of Military Force in the Absence of Justice

As we have demonstrated, injustice is important because it serves to generate feelings of humiliation, alienation, frustration, and anger. It is not hard to grasp that alienation, combined with frustration and anger, can lead people to engage in extreme actions in an attempt to regain agency. Employing military force alone in an effort to increase security will not be fruitful if real or perceived injustice by groups, states, sub-national or supranational non-state cultures persists. Not only will the root causes of the particular issue at hand continue to fester, but those who wish to propagate insecurity and instability will find fertile ground for their ideas in places where people feel that their agency cannot be expressed through other mechanisms.

(b) Marginalizing Extremism Through the Pursuit of Justice

Considerations of justice are imperative when analyzing security challenges and when devising policies aimed at meeting them. The only way to marginalize and render extreme groups redundant is to remove the basis of their appeal to the masses. This can only be achieved through sustained and comprehensive efforts to reduce injustice in whatever form it appears. While there will always be extreme elements in societies, their appeal to the masses will be ineffective and of little purchase if justice is understood as a prerequisite of security and rigorously pursued. Without justice, no amount of public-relations strategies will work, nor will the resort to the use of force guarantee enduring security.

(c) Justice as a Prerequisite for Security

Understanding justice as a prerequisite for security implies a number of things. First, people's intrinsic worth has to be recognized. This means that governments should treat all people with equal concern and respect. They should not distribute rights or opportunities on an unequal basis. This implies that governments should act on the assumption that all individuals are of equal worth in and of themselves. Yet, the mere idea that all human beings have unconditional worth does not tell us what kinds of treatment fail to show consideration of that intrinsic worth. The abstract ideal of the dignity of all needs to be given content by reference to what constitutes a violation of human dignity.

Second, states, as well as multilateral institutions, must make it their priority to foster understanding of, and respect for, people's sense of identity and dignity, as well as their ethnic, cultural, and religious diversity. This is vital if we are to reduce the number of instances of defining and treating people as inferior to others, which, as mentioned, prevents them from expressing their true selves. Commonalities rather than differences ought to be promoted through education, responsible political statements, and the sensitization of media professionals to prejudices and stereotyping.

Third, since alienation is a fundamental expression of injustice, which can lead to tension and violence, it is essential for governments and multilateral institutions to strive to reduce the structural causes of inequalities and alienation within and between states and regions. At the state level, this requires governments to increase access to resources and opportunities for all, which should follow on from recognition of the inherent worth of all human beings. At the regional and global levels, it means creating fair rules for trade and capital flows, as well as equitable representation within global political institutions, e.g., through reform of the UN Security Council.

Fourth, it is imperative that states respect international law and obligations in order to reduce perceptions of injustice within the international system that can lead to animosity. This is important because a state's refusal to be bound by the International Criminal Court is likely to signal to other states and individuals that justice will be selective. The selective application of justice is likely to sow the seeds for further local frustration, dissent, and opposition. However, if considerations of justice were to inform policy making, international law and international obligations would be respected. Consequently, antagonism and mistrust would be replaced by confidence in the good faith and credibility of others. Moreover, fewer people would be motivated to engage in extreme actions in an attempt to alter the international balance of power relations.

Fifth, the most obvious way in which to minimize perceptions of injustice, alienation, frustration, and anger is to empower people. This is because injustice causes alienation, and alienation contributes to security problems because it robs people of their agency to define themselves and their lives. Policy makers should, therefore, include participants from all sides of the debate or conflict in order to generate comprehensive understanding of, and responses to, challenges. In doing so, they should be sensitive to perceptions of people from other cultural contexts. While the temptation for states to conduct their policies on the basis of narrowly defined, short-term self-interests may be great, the policies of responsible states aim to be comprehensive. Indeed, it is in their own long-term self-interest to ensure that this is the case. In order to avoid feeding perceptions of injustice, states should also eschew practices that may be perceived as hypocritical.

4. Conclusion

In this chapter, we focused on the security implications of injustice and the significance of justice to the advancement of global security. We argued that, while justice is a fundamental security concern, it is all too often ignored by policy makers, or it is viewed as a philosophical rather than national-security question. As we have highlighted, however, many security challenges are at some level spawned by injustice in one form or another. Specifically, injustice is important because it serves to generate feelings of humiliation, frustration, and anger. For this reason, justice constitutes a vital dimension of our proposed new security principle, **the multi-sum security principle**.

First, we began by briefly looking at the concept of justice, stressing its context-specific nature. Second, we examined the relationship between real or perceived injustice and feelings of frustration, anger, and humiliation. Third, we suggested that such sentiments are generated by alienation, which may provoke extreme forms of action. Fourth, we briefly examined some contemporary examples of the how real or perceived injustice can lead to feelings of humiliation, alienation, frustration, and anger. And, finally, we argued that justice is imperative if lasting security and stability are to be achieved.

Based on this reasoning, we claimed that attempting to deal with many security problems by resorting to the use of military force will be ineffective as long as real or perceived injustice continues to exist. This is because people who feel alienated also feel dispossessed of their agency, and as long as this is the case, they will use whatever means available to them to try to regain it and to be faithful to their true evaluative commitments. Moreover, as long as injustices persist, people who wish to propagate insecurity and instability will find an audience for their ideas, no matter how illogical, futile, or violent. Therefore, without justice, long-term security will be ephemeral.

Respect for people's equal worth, whether in terms of identity, dignity, or their cultural, ethnic, and religious diversity, is vital to promoting greater justice. This should also be combined with efforts to reduce structural economic and political inequalities that contribute to alienation and possible conflict. Of course, one of the most vital things to understand when promoting greater justice is the significance of empowerment. People are driven to extremes because they cannot express their frustrations, their anger, their hopes, and their fears through regular political channels. The attainment of justice allows people to regain their full agency as human beings capable of defining themselves and their lives in a way that is authentic to them.

CHAPTER 5

THE MULTI-SUM SECURITY PRINCIPLE

1. Introduction

In the last chapter, we focused on the security implications of injustice and the significance of justice to the enhancement of global security. Specifically, we argued that injustice is central to understanding insecurity because it generates feelings of alienation. This, we explained, dispossesses people of their agency. The implications of this are highly relevant to security. As long as people feel that they cannot express themselves through regular channels, they will resort to whatever means are available to them in order to be faithful to their evaluative commitments. Furthermore, if injustices are left unaddressed, they will provide fodder for those who seek to propagate insecurity and instability. Therefore, we concluded that, without justice, security will be short-lived, and that justice is imperative for lasting security and stability.

In this chapter, we set out our proposed security principle, which we hope will contribute to enhancing security through justice for all individuals, states, and cultures. This principle is called the ***multi-sum security principle***, which suggests that, in a globalized world, security should not be thought of as a zero-sum game involving states alone. Rather, it involves human, environmental, national, transnational, and transcultural security, in which the security of individuals, states, and cultures cannot be achieved without justice through good governance at all levels. It is based on a fusion of our proposed classification of global security and the imperative of justice for long-term security within one framework. Then, we explore the linkage between injustice and insecurity within the five dimensions of global security outlined in Chapter 3, namely human, environmental, national, transnational, and transcultural security.

2. The Multi-sum Security Principle

(a) The Five Dimensions of Global Security

At the very outset of this book, we suggested a classification of global security that consisted of five substrates: human, environmental, national, transnational, and transcultural security. Our aim in doing so is to contribute to a more comprehensive approach to security. This follows on the heels of efforts to develop a more all-embracing vision of security in the years subsequent to the end of the Cold War when the concept of security went through a process of both widening and deepening.

To recap, the state is the referent object (i.e., that which is to be secured) in the realist security paradigm. This means that security essentially refers to the security of the state. Since the state is the highest political authority in the international system, securing the integrity of the state has both internal and external dimensions. Internally, the state must possess the capacity to enforce its laws. Externally, it must be able to ensure its territorial integrity. Thus, the use of force is intimately linked to the nature of statehood. As a result, all variants of realism contend that states strive for military (and sometimes economic) power in order to secure their survival.

This assumption has several implications. First, with no higher authority with which to guarantee their security, security competition between a plurality of states makes the international state system a self-help system. In such a system, no state can be absolutely sure that its security will be guaranteed by any other body. The assumed rationality of states means that each can be expected to pursue similar goals in order to secure itself within an inherently insecure system. The pursuit of security is a zero-sum struggle for power, largely defined in military terms.

Second, given the security competition within the state system, states are thought to be unable to agree on universal principles, except that of non-intervention. The skeptical interpretation of human nature and the motivation of states also means that moral considerations in international relations are assumed to be subordinate to the imperative of survival and the resulting pursuit of power. While realists do not entirely exclude the possibility of moral considerations in state policy, the egoistic passions of people or the constraints of anarchy in international politics win out.

Third, realists diverge on the question of whether states can escape the constraints imposed on them by the security dilemma. Classical realists argue that the security dilemma can be minimized through the balance of power. Structural realists believe that it is an enduring characteristic of the international system. Maintaining a balance of power became a central objective in the foreign policies of the Great Powers. All agree, however, that balances of power are not stable. Moreover, egoism, whether the result of human nature or the anarchical structure of the international system, mitigates against the provision of collective goods, such as collective security. Alliances and cooperative arrangements between states are unlikely to last. In addition, institutions are not thought to have a significant impact on the dynamics of the inter-state system. They are viewed as the product of state interest and the constraints imposed upon them by the anarchical international system.

In contrast to this view, other approaches to international security exist that take power politics seriously, but that also leave room for domestic politics, norms, and beliefs to inform international politics. Proponents of **collective security** hold that, while military force remains an important characteristic of international life, the formal anarchical structure of the international system need not necessarily lead to a security dilemma for states. According to them, the international state system has developed rules and practices that guide state-to-state relations and enable a certain degree of order to evolve. The League of Nations constituted a prominent example of the concept of collective security in practice. It was perceived as a government of governments, settling disputes between individual states in an open and legalistic manner.

Despite the tremendous contribution of collective security in practice, manifested, for example, in the UN, the concept of collective security was considered too narrow to meet the security challenges that states now face, such as the environment, organized criminality, and terrorism. While "high" politics, involving military (and, in some instances, economic) issues in traditional conflicts between states are important, low" politics are also significant security concerns. What this means is that the state should no longer be given priority as a referent object of security. Consequently, an increasing number of IR scholars, including some neo-realists, called for a widening of the security agenda. Buzan, Waever, and de Wilde, for example, proposed a sectoral approach to security that identified five principal sectors, or substrates, of security: military, political, economic, environmental, and societal. In the military sector, the referent object of security is typically the state, though it may also be other types of political entity.

While the Copenhagen School made a significant contribution to Security Studies, it did not fully break with realism's state-centrism. The sectoral approach did enable something other than the state to be a referent object of security. Yet, within this framework, the state was identified as a security provider.

Other approaches to security, however, departed even further from the realist security paradigm, contending that the individual rather than the state should be the primary referent object of security. As a result, human security was proposed as a competing security paradigm. The concept was defined and employed primarily within the context of the UN system. Human security, according to the UNDP, may be defined as freedom from want and freedom from fear. Within this paradigm, threats to human security may be linked to economic, food, health, environmental, personal, community, or political security. Therefore, enhancing human security requires a multifaceted approach. Despite the fact that it is often criticized for being too inclusive and vague, the concept is attractive because of its capacity to capture the various factors that reduce individual security.

The ***cooperative-security concept*** incorporates dimensions of all of these approaches. It implies more than collective security in that it involves achieving security *with* others rather than against them. In addition, it also goes beyond collective security in that it not only looks inward, ensuring security and stability within a cooperative security zone, but also outward. Looking outward implies promoting stability outside the cooperative security space, in the near abroad or even further afield. Indeed, trouble spots in far-flung areas of the globe have become a serious security concern in an age of intensified transnational challenges to security. According to Richard Cohen, cooperative security must also include human security. Indeed, from this perspective, the security of the individual is the foundation upon which all other security depends. In a world of growing interconnectivity, the human condition has become a common and basic concern, making the Westphalian concept of non-interference less tenable. What this implies is that states can, in fact, agree on ethical principles. It assumes not only that states can engage in lasting cooperation, but that their security depends upon it.[213] Therefore, security is no longer considered a zero-sum game. This is important, since security through cooperation is imperative in a world in which threats to security are often transnational in nature. While sharing the same conviction that states can engage in cooperative relations and, in so doing, significantly improve their security, it goes beyond the collective-security concept in that cooperation involves various kinds of collaborative activities aimed at responding to a variety of security challenges, many of which are non-military in nature and require non-military responses.

In an effort to provide an even more inclusive view of global security, we proposed a new classification of global security in Chapter 2, including five substrates of global security: **human, environmental, national, transnational, and transcultural.** The first is human security, which, as mentioned, refers to the security of individuals. The second is environmental security, which refers to the security of the biosphere. The third is national security, referring to the state's population, economic situation, and organizational integrity. The fourth, transnational security, involves security against transnational threats that refer to any type of illegal transborder phenomenon. These four referents were largely present in the sectoral and cooperative-security approaches and in the human-security paradigm. Yet, the impact and implications of transnational security challenges are multi-faceted and far-reaching, and responses to such threats must be similar in scope, applicability, and complexity. The fifth substrate of security is transcultural security, which refers to ensuring that a plurality of cultures and civilizations can coexist without their relations being elevated to security issues. Our classification, therefore, goes beyond the realist security paradigm in an additional sense: It brings culture onto center stage, whereas realism has traditionally marginalized it.

The sectoral approach addressed this to some extent. Indeed, societal security was perhaps the biggest contribution the approach made to Security Studies. The identification of the security of groups and cultures within states is particularly important within the context of transnational realities, including migration and irregular immigration and xenophobic and exclusionary tendencies in host societies with regard to race, political beliefs, and religion. Societal security implies that there are large-scale collective identities that are not necessarily lined up with the state. Societal security is related to, but distinct from, political security, which refers to the stability of the system of government, institutions, and sometimes ideology that lend governments their legitimacy. In the societal approach, large-scale collective identities can exist independently from the state and vary in time and space.[214]

Whether societal security becomes an issue will, according to Buzan, Waever, and De Wilde, depend on how collective identities respond to external or internal developments. This, in turn, is likely to depend on whether the holders of a collective identity take a closed-minded or open-minded view of how their identity is constituted and maintained.[215] Collective identities are most often perceived to be under threat in relation to issues such as migration, horizontal competition with a neighboring culture, vertical competition (e.g., regional integration), and perhaps depopulation as a result of disease, war, famine, natural catastrophe, or policies of extermination.[216]

With our fifth substrate of global security, transcultural security, we identify cultures and civilizations as referent objects. Earlier, we defined culture as a refined awareness of the religious tradition, customs, and the institutional and aesthetic achievements of a nation or group. It is the framework on which civilizations, which refers to advanced systems of social organization, are built.[217]

In our view, there needs to be a balance, a synergy found within cultural and broader civilizational variations, even if competition and non-violent conflict can sometimes generate improvements in the human condition. At the level of the international political community, alliance-building and the coexistence of civilizations are vital when dealing with transnational threats to security. This is particularly the case in an age of intensified transcultural interaction. When acting together, individual cultures can have a greater impact on global security than any individual culture could when acting independently. Thus, a plurality of cultures can have a net effect on global security that is greater than would be the case if representatives of individual cultures acted individually. This, we might think of as transcultural synergy. Transcultural security is a vital component of enhancing security globally, with the eventual goal of achieving transcultural synergy.

To summarize, we suggest that global security should be viewed as comprising five substrates: **human, environmental, national, transnational, and transcultural security**. While these five aspects of security are, of course, interlinked, separating them analytically is useful insofar as it takes into account a variety of referent objects of security, as well as a variety of means with which to achieve security. The latter are likely to be wide-ranging. However, we contended in the previous chapter that justice is fundamental to achieving long-term security.

(b) Justice as a Prerequisite for Security

Justice, at both the state and global levels, should be a fundamental consideration when formulating security policies, negotiating an end to conflict, or rebuilding in post-conflict environments. While this may appear obvious, the question of justice has been woefully neglected by traditional Security Studies and policy makers alike. This means that a significant source of animosity among states and within communities has gone unattended.

As mentioned, part of the reason for this shortcoming is related to the dominance of political realism and its tendency to relegate ethical concerns to the domestic realm. We take a different view. Ethical principles can, and to some extent already do, regulate state behavior and dampen the negative implications of international anarchy through the creation of rules of conduct and institutions with which to guide behavior. Indeed, in our view, enhancing global security depends on giving greater expression to ethical principles not only within the domestic sphere but also globally.

Efforts to correct injustices have led to the creation of rights and institutions in the domestic realm. Injustice on a global scale now refers to a range of issues from the gap between rich and poor to the vulnerability of people to abuse, violence, occupation, exclusion, humiliation, disease, and starvation. What justice may imply is, however, likely to depend on the specifics of a particular issue. It may refer to fairness, wrongs done to others and what those people or groups may claim from the perpetrators, what people are due, or redress for past wrongs.

Injustice is important because it generates feelings of humiliation, frustration, and anger. This can result in the alienation of people from the societies and institutions that they are supposedly a part of. If those societies, whether domestic or international, fail to address injustices, military force alone will not guarantee security. As long as real or perceived injustices are left to fester, people will be motivated to engage in extreme acts in an attempt to redress injustices. People intent on propagating insecurity and instability will fill the vacuum left by mainstream outlets for frustration. This is because people who feel alienated as a result of injustice also feel divested of their agency, and they are likely to be willing to use whatever means available to them to try to influence their lives and the things they hold dear. The only way to remove the appeal of such actions is to promote greater justice. Tension and conflict will be mitigated if justice is understood as a prerequisite of security and is rigorously pursued. Without justice, security will be short-lived.

Recognition of people's equal worth, whether in terms of individual or collective identity, is vital to reducing sentiments of alienation and enhancing justice. This means that empowerment is central to the promotion of greater justice. Instead of expressing their frustrations, anger, hopes, and fears by engaging in extreme actions, people will be more likely to do so using regular channels of communication. The attainment of justice necessarily implies empowerment, since it allows people to regain their full agency as human beings insofar as it enables them to define themselves and their lives in ways that are authentic to them. Justice, therefore, forms a central dimension of our proposed new security principle, which we hope will contribute to long-term global security.

(c) The Multi-sum Security Principle
Our proposed principle is presented in figure 2 (which appears on page 31) in the form of a pentagon. It takes this form because, as mentioned, our classification of global security comprises five types of security: **human, environmental, national, transnational, and transcultural security,** each of which appears in a separate rectangle within the diagram. In our view, advancing each of these five aspects of security depends on the promotion of justice. For this reason, our multi-sum security principle, which appears within the pentagon depicted in the diagram, has the pursuit of justice at its core. What justice entails will depend on the specific issue being addressed.

3. Multi-sum Security in Practice

In this section, we explore the relationship between injustice and insecurity within the five substrates of security that comprise our classification of global security: human, environmental, national, transnational, and transcultural security. The issues discussed are by no means exhaustive and are simply intended to illustrate the importance of justice to enhancing security.

(a) Justice and Human Security

One type of justice that is relevant to reducing human insecurities is social justice. While the transnationalization of production and services and technological developments are creating new job opportunities, the processes associated with globalization are unfolding in the absence of a universal concern for justice.

Mainstream Security Studies has traditionally obscured the issue of class. Nonetheless, differential socioeconomic positions are critical to determining the satisfaction of human needs, since inequalities stemming from disparities in social power manifest themselves in various forms of exploitation, subordination, and unequal access to resources.

Inequalities of wealth manifest themselves in relation to health, poverty, mortality, and education.[218] At one level, economic liberalization is premised on the belief that the market will ensure the optimal allocation of resources. But this masks the distortions caused by unequal social power. For example, medical technology exists to prevent many diseases from being fatal. Yet, many people will die as a result of contracting these diseases, either because the logic of economic liberalization does not encourage an urgent response to them or because access is restricted to those who can afford adequate treatment.

Satisfying human needs depends on good governance. When it does not exist, ruling elites may adhere to the interests of those members of society with the greatest social power. This does not mean that governments simply cater to the interests of powerful domestic or transnational class groupings, but that the interests of the state and dominant class often tend to mesh together. In the absence of, for example, transparency and accountability, powerful social forces may use state power to defend their own narrow interests. Equally, a lack of participation of the people is likely to bring about policies that are not comprehensive and that therefore fail to address the basic needs of many. Bad governance is also likely to restrict the possibilities of people to contest the authority of the government or to demand that resources be used in a way that benefits the whole of society. This can lead people to experience alienation from the societies in which they live.

The relationship between justice and human security is also apparent in post-conflict situations. After conflict has ceased, societies often lack the mechanisms and institutions for upholding the rule of law and dealing with past abuses, both of which are essential to the process of rebuilding. Indeed, Michèle Flournoy and Michael Pan argue in their article "Dealing with Demons: Justice and Reconciliation" that "Justice and reconciliation, in tandem, must be seen as a central pillar of any assistance for post-conflict reconstruction and should receive priority attention early and throughout the life of an operation."[219] Justice is an integral part of the reconciliation process upon which a more peaceful future can be built.

Past atrocities and grievances need to be addressed, either in post-conflict societies or in countries that have undergone regime change. This is an issue of justice because it involves the perception of past behavior constituting unforgivable acts. Failure to address past grievances can lead to a loss of gains in terms of human security, since the perpetrators of previous abuses and crime may be still at large. As mentioned during our discussion of justice in Chapter 4, a dilemma frequently exists between the non-violent coexistence and justice. Yet, international law has evolved enough to ensure that war crimes are increasingly subject to indictment, prosecution, and punishment. Addressing forms of past discrimination and abuse may involve establishing processes aimed at holding people accountable for them, without being punished. Criminal prosecution may be foregone in favor of documenting, acknowledging, and condemning past behavior.

This requires emergency justice measures aimed at rapidly establishing a provisional justice system to provide for public security. At the same time, international actors need to assist with the creation of indigenous processes and institutions for the administration of justice. Justice should also be accessible to the population at large. Immediate attention should also be given to addressing abuses that occurred during a conflict, such as gross violations of human rights and mass killings. This is the only way in which communities can be healed and individuals empowered.[220]

(b) Justice and Environmental Security

As Yozo Yokata notes in "International Justice and the Global Environment":

> A body of international law requiring sovereign states to regulate behavior that affects the environment has not yet been well developed. In light of this, some states claim that they have complete and independent authority over deciding if and how they should implement environmental policies. The national and international impact of environmental policies dictates that justice con-

cerns play an integral role in this policymaking process. Even so, the responses of governments to environmental problems may differ depending on their respective interpretations of justice. Because justice can be defined in many ways, states must agree upon an exact meaning in order to provide consensual solutions to environmental questions.[221]

What it means to pursue justice in relation to environmental security is perhaps the most challenging to define. Yokata suggests three reasons why we should consider problems resulting from environmental change matters of justice. First, to be just to future generations who will inherit the Earth. This kind of intergenerational justice requires that we do our best to make sure that, for instance, our children and grandchildren do not suffer from high rates of skin cancer as a result of depletion of the ozone layer. Second, justice may refer to the other species with which we share the planet. Third, justice may refer to recourse for those who suffer in a direct and immediate way from environmental degradation.[222]

Many people would also argue that the environment has some intrinsic value in and of itself and that we should be concerned with it not simply because we view it as just another instrumental facet of human welfare, such as food or shelter. This implies that it should be given privileged weight in assessing the contribution of environmental preservation to human welfare. This would affect both any comparison between the effect of alternative policies on the welfare of future generations as against the welfare of the current generation, and the assessment of how much the present generation should devote to environmental protection as against other claims on resources.[223]

Several difficulties arise when dealing with the question of whether the biosphere is the bearer of some intrinsic value. Should it be viewed as having intrinsic value independent of any human evaluation? It could be argued that nature has an objective value, because of its beauty and harmony, for instance. But beauty and harmony are subjective qualities. They necessarily relate to the value that individuals attach to them.[224]

A potential problem that could be encountered when discussing the relevance of justice to environmental security is the uncertainty surrounding some global environmental issues. For example, there is no consensus among scientists as to the precise causal relationship between global climate change and increases in greenhouse-gas emissions. As a result, policy makers promoting greater justice in relation to environmental security may find it difficult to be effective without firm scientific evidence supporting the causal relationship between human activity and environmental degradation.[225]

(c) Justice and National Security

Justice is fundamental to the political dimension of national security. The political security of a state – defined earlier as the stability of institutionalized authority – is related to matters of justice. The legitimacy of state authority will depend on equal representation of the people. This implies universal suffrage and the holding of democratic elections. A major shortcoming of some of the most established democracies is the influence of money on electoral outcomes. Campaign-finance reform may be required in certain instances to change the involvement of money in politics, principally in electoral campaigns. Although there have been efforts to regulate campaign finance through legislation, laws are not always adequately enforced, and there is often no independent central agency to enforce them. The most effective way of reducing the influence of money in the electoral system is arguably to provide public financing for political campaigns in order to level the playing field. Checks and balances within the political system through a separation of the powers between the parliamentary bodies and the government should also be ensured. In addition, strict limits on terms of office should be established in order to avoid abuse of power.

Political security is dependent on justice in that it requires law-enforcement instruments not only to be effective, but also to be respectful of civil liberties and human rights. The freedom of speech is an essential civil liberty that contributes to the stability of institutionalized authority. From our point of view, respect for this freedom implies that everyone has the right to say or write whatever they wish without censorship or risk of punishment, as long as they do not incite hatred or violence. It is also essential that the media be able to contribute to public dissent in a state. Unfortunately, the spirit of public criticism is often compromised, even in the most established democracies, as a result of the influence of politics and money. People should also enjoy other basic civil liberties, such as the freedom of assembly, people's right to petition their governments for a redress of grievances, as well as the right to secure themselves, their houses, and effects against unreasonable or arbitrary searches and seizures.

An impartial, open, and accountable judicial system is also essential to the political security of a state. Equality before the law should be accompanied by greater equality in general. Therefore, governments should strive to reduce structural inequalities related to ethnicity, class, and gender. A state that fails to treat all of its citizens according to their equal worth is likely to suffer from challenges to its sovereignty not only from within, but also from without. The increasing acceptance of human-rights norms within the international community represents a reformulation of the traditional understanding of state sovereignty. If a state fails to respect the human rights of a particular community within its society, its political security may be threatened as a result of an intervention by the international community. Those states that respect their constituent communities are less likely to experience such a challenge to their political security through contestations of, for instance, the national ideal. The political security of the state will therefore be enhanced by the existence of mechanisms for monitoring and upholding human rights.[226]

The stability of institutionalized authority also requires the prudent use of resources that collectively belong to the people. This implies minimizing waste and eliminating corruption and inefficiencies that prevent resources from being allocated to serve the needs and respond to the demands of the people. Mechanisms should be in place that people can use to hold their governments accountable for the allocation of resources. Accountability also depends on access to reliable and timely information about government activities. Transparency should therefore be energetically pursued in order to preclude conflicts of interest and the buying of influence.

The economic dimension of national security overlaps somewhat with human security in that it requires a certain degree of social justice, given that it involves the state ensuring the well-being of the population. Governments that fail to provide for the basic sustenance of the population are also likely to suffer from challenges to their political security, productivity, and growth.

(d) Justice and Transnational Security

While we believe that *international terrorism is completely unacceptable, whatever its causes*, an examination of terrorism may help demonstrate the relevance of justice to transnational security. We mentioned in Chapter 3 that changes in the international system have facilitated the emergence and consolidation of international terrorist groups motivated by religious extremism. A number of contemporary terrorist organizations operate transnationally, establishing operational bases across national boundaries and moving from one country to another. Indeed, transnational terrorist groups have neither a particular territorial home country that they are seeking to liberate nor a homeland to be used as a base. As such, they represent a transnational security challenge.

While international terrorism creates security challenges that are transnational in character, its root causes are partly traceable to the turmoil of a modern and globalizing international system. It is at least in part facilitated by new technological and communications networks and societal reactions to a seemingly unjust and largely economic form of globalization that disseminate a global culture that may appear threatening to local ways of life and cultural heritages. Increased access to media coverage of events in remote regions of the world has also enabled people to compare their lot with that of others.

Justice is relevant to international terrorism in that, for the poor and underprivileged, the life situations of the affluent must appear highly unjust. Terrorist groups flourish on the failure of states, as well as the international community, to deliver basic services, social justice, and growing economies that bring opportunities for all rather than just a select few. It also thrives on the failure of states to manage peaceful change and on the failure of economies to adapt to demographic shifts. Increased exposure through the media and new technologies to events elsewhere in the world has also increased people's knowledge of injustices related to political oppression, abuse, and discrimination. International terrorists fill the vacuum created by alienation, anger, and frustration by offering an opportunity to alter the situation at some future point.

In order to address the root causes of international terrorism, states must cooperate with each other in a number of areas. Cooperation may take the form of diplomatic support for one another, intelligence-sharing, law-enforcement cooperation, and initiatives to alleviate poverty and to institutionalize economic reforms. The international community should focus on the social, economic, and political causes of terrorism. Above all, addressing international terrorism requires patience and the formulation of an international strategy that addresses perceived and actual injustices and fills the vacuum that terrorist groups based on religious fundamentalism exploit. Such efforts need to be synchronized with a reformulation of states' foreign-policy priorities and approaches.[227]

No anti-terrorism campaign that relies on military means alone will succeed in delivering lasting security and stability if questions of justice are left unattended. This is because people who wish to propagate insecurity and instability will find fertile ground for their warped ideas in places where injustice exists. Marginalizing extreme groups implies promoting greater justice in the world. While there will always be extreme elements in societies, their attraction will be minimized if justice is understood as a prerequisite of security and is rigorously pursued.

(e) Justice and Transcultural Security
Shortly after the end of the Cold War, Samuel Huntington proclaimed that the greatest fault line in the 21st century would be between civilizations. In short, Huntington suggested that our fate would be shaped by a "clash of civilizations."[228] Framing the relations between civilizations in this way essentially implies, as Richard Bulliet notes, that "Civilizations that are fated to clash cannot forge a common future."[229]

Today, in the aftermath of September 11, 2001, and the "problems" that Western European countries have with their Muslim communities, Huntington's polemic may seem appealing, even if highly facile. But it is important to recognize that the appeal of this proposition stems from a narrative that characterizes the West's common history with Islam in largely conflictual terms, highlighting key events such as the fall of Crusader Jerusalem to Saladin in 1187, the fall of Byzantine Constantinople to the Ottomans in 1453, and the near successful siege of Vienna in 1529. The undercurrent of this narrative suggests that Muslims have always been conspiring to carry out violent political acts apparently based on religious principles.

Faced with a professedly resurgent Muslim Other, the Judeo-Christian civilization appears under threat. Yet, as Bulliet points out, neither the Muslim nor the Christian historical trajectory can be fully understood in isolation from the other. For example, many Orthodox Christians lived under Ottoman rule for several centuries and, as a result, Muslim thinkers drew heavily on Orthodox Christianity's Greek heritage.[230] Moreover, the notion of a Judeo-Christian civilization is in many respects paradoxical, given that the common history of Jews and Christians is replete with a good deal of tragedy.

Depicting communities of difference as malevolent Others is almost certain to decrease security and increase insecurity, since the act of defining other collective identities in a way that detracts from their worth will undoubtedly generate feelings of alienation, anger, and frustration. This is because it dispossesses their members of the agency to define themselves in a way that they can identify with. For instance, Western critics of Islam frequently ask whether Muslims can "meet" the civilizational standards of the West. Framing the issues in this way does a number of things. First, it obscures the failures of the West to live up to its own standards.[231] Second, it assumes that the values of the West are inherently superior to those of the Muslim world. Not surprisingly, this creates frustration and anger and a sense of injustice among Muslims, since it defines their cultural heritage (an intrinsic part of self-identity) in a way that is denigrating and leaves little opportunity for Muslims to alter an image of themselves that is alien to them. As long as feelings of injustice continue, those intent on propagating insecurity and instability will succeed in doing so.

Today, people belonging to different cultures have much more contact with one another than they did in the Middle Ages. In countries undergoing rapid transformation as a result of modernization and globalization, exposure to Western consumer preferences and culture diffused through advanced communications technology can sometimes cause defensive reactions as people feel that their way of life and cultural heritage is under threat. Moreover, as a result of migratory movements, large Muslim communities now reside in almost every country in the world, including those of Western Europe and North America.[232] Against this backdrop, people should be wary of easy formulations about distant Others that may risk generating divisions and antagonisms. We would do well to recognize that the most significant fault lines are within societies rather than between civilizations and that communities of difference can be a source of creativity when inclusion is affirmed.

Thus, justice is central to transcultural security. Respect for people's equal worth, whether in terms of identity, dignity, or their cultural, ethnic, and religious diversity is vital to promoting greater justice.

4. Conclusion

In this chapter, we began by proposing a new security principle, which we called the ***multi-sum security principle***. This draws together our proposed classification of global security, which comprises five aspects of security – **human, environmental, national, transnational, and transcultural security** – and the notion that justice is a requisite for security. The multi-sum security principle states that: **"In a globalized world, security can no longer be thought of as a zero-sum game involving states alone. Global security, instead, has five dimensions that include human, environmental, national, transnational, and transcultural security, and, therefore, global security and the security of any state or culture cannot be achieved without good governance at all levels that guarantees security through *justice* for *all* individuals, states, and cultures."**

We then explored the relationship between injustice and insecurity within the five substrates of global security. We found that one of the most vital things to understand when promoting greater justice is the significance of empowerment. People are driven to extremes because they cannot express their frustrations, anger, hopes, and fears through the usual political channels. The pursuit of justice is central to security, because it restores people's capacity to defining themselves and their lives in a way that fits with their evaluative commitments.

CHAPTER 6

GOOD GOVERNANCE

1. Introduction

In the last chapter, we brought our proposed classification of global security and the relevance of justice for long-term security together in order to propose a more comprehensive approach to global security. Specifically, we outlined our *multi-sum security principle*. We then explored the linkage between justice and security within the five substrates of global security (human, environmental, national, transnational, and transcultural security). In this chapter, we focus on the centrality of good governance (domestic, regional, and global) to global security. Governance is frequently taken to refer, among other things, to public-sector management, accountability, a functioning legal system, openness, and freedom of information. The term itself is often used to refer to "democratic governance," based on the tenets of Western political theory. Not surprisingly, therefore, the term "good governance" is viewed with a considerable degree of misgiving in many non-Western parts of the world where a considerable degree of suspicion about the motives behind the promotion of good governance may exist or where its applicability beyond the West is questioned. Nevertheless, good governance, as we understand it, serves as an important means of enhancing security not simply in developing countries and countries in transition from communism, but also in mature democracies that are falling short in this area.

In our view, good governance requires a set of overlapping authority structures and public-policy frameworks at the local, state, regional, and wider global levels. At the local level, direct participatory processes may exist, with state, regional, and global levels mediating political engagement through representative, open, and accountable institutions and mechanisms. Contestation over the correct jurisdiction of different levels of governance is bound to be complex, but as David Held comments: "better complex and intensive in a clear public framework than left simply to powerful geopolitical interests (dominant states) or market-based organizations to resolve them alone."[233] Participation is an essential criterion for good governance, since it helps to ensure that the mobilization of political power will be used to express needs, demand responses, and to hold officials to account. Clearly, the participation of all actors concerned with a particular problem needs to be guaranteed, as well as subsidiarity wherever possible, in order to ensure that comprehensive solutions are found.[234] Primacy of cosmopolitan law should ensure "the protection of man, of his rights and of his dignity."[235] Policies ought to also promote mutual recognition and respect as a means of bringing people together.

We begin by discussing good governance at the domestic level, which, today, entails protection of basic civil and human rights; institutions that are representative, transparent, and accountable; and inclusivity. We then suggest that good regional and global governance structures should exist in order to complement those at the state and local levels. At the regional level, governance structures should be inclusive, open, and accountable. At the global level, good governance implies the primacy of an expansive form of cosmopolitan international law, multilateral cooperation backed up by cosmopolitan international law, and effective multilateral institutions.

2. Good Domestic Governance

(a) Protection of Civil and Human Rights

Good governance, of course, involves respect for basic civil liberties. Freedom of speech is an essential civil liberty that contributes to good governance. Everyone should be able to say or write what they wish, so long as they do not incite hatred or violence. The press should be free and independent from outside influence, again insofar as ethical codes of conduct are established, preferably on a voluntary basis. It is essential that the media be able to contribute to the spirit of public dissent in a country. Unfortunately, freedom of the press is often compromised, even in some of the most mature democracies, as a result of political influence, increasing concentration of media ownership, and the merger of media organizations with non-media organizations.[236] For the media to contribute fully to good governance, it should be free from the influence of money and power. People should also enjoy civil rights, such as the right of assembly; the right to petition their governments for redress of grievances; the right to secure themselves, their houses, and effects against unreasonable or arbitrary searches and seizures; the right to a speedy and fair trial; and equality before the law.

Yet, civil liberties alone are not sufficient to ensure good governance. Protection of basic human rights must also be ensured. These rights belong to people simply by virtue of their being human beings. The term "right" can mean a number of different things. On the one hand, it can refer to what is morally correct. On the other hand, it can also refer to what someone is due. It is in the latter sense that people have human rights. This distinction is an important one to make. Rights that refer to something that is morally correct are related to natural-law theories within the Western philosophical tradition. Natural-law theories are premised on the idea that there exists an objective moral law, either given by God or by human reason. Historically, theories of natural law were important in that they provided means for citizens to protect themselves against the state, since rulers who violated natural law were believed to have transgressed objective moral laws and would thus be held accountable to God. Human rights, however, provide a more concrete basis upon which to claim redress in the event of their violation. Whereas a ruler violating natural law was considered guilty of moral crimes according to theories of natural law, governments violating human rights are guilty of violating their own *citizens'* rights that are codified in law.

Human rights are, of course, universal, since they are rights that every person possesses simply by being human. The universal nature of human rights may, however, be qualified for a number of reasons. First, the form in which human rights are institutionalized may be subject to cultural specificities. Second, the specification of human rights will reflect the concerns of the era in which they were drafted.[237]

(b) Inclusion (Socioeconomic, Cultural, and Political)
Good governance implies respect not only for civil and human rights, but also for inclusivity. Respect for, and tolerance of, cultural, ethnic, and religious diversity, as well as people's sense of dignity and identity are essential elements of good governance. The "race" riots in northern England, the murder of Dutch filmmaker Theo Van Gogh, the urban unrest in France, and the reaction to the publication of the Mohammed cartoons in Denmark underscore the centrality of inclusion to good governance. These examples emphasize, in particular, the

difficulties that societies can have in managing relations between diverse cultural groups and avoiding the marginalization of any specific group. Moreover, a lack of recognition and respect for the cultural heritage of minority groups is often coupled with socioeconomic inequalities and a lack of political representation. Political and socioeconomic inequalities structured along ethnic or cultural lines will almost inevitably lead to alienation, frustration, and anger.

Respect for, and tolerance of, diversity is likely to encourage innovation and dynamism within a society. Those countries that are more successful in managing cultural pluralism will be better equipped to reap the benefits of diversity. Awareness and recognition of diversity are prerequisites for the construction of a society built on mutual respect and tolerance. This does not mean, however, that the views and practices of others must be accepted at all costs; it implies engagement with others and respect for other "truths." Contact with difference, however difficult, can be a source of stimulation and dynamism. It is also likely to generate more comprehensive policy responses. Including people from different cultural groups in political processes is also important.

Recognition of, and respect for, cultural differences should also be accompanied by greater equality in general. Governments should strive to reduce structural inequalities related to class and gender, in addition to those linked to race and ethnicity. Effectively addressing these issues demands long-term, multifaceted, and comprehensive approaches to reducing inequalities. Greater equality needs to be institutionalized, partly through the empowerment of those groups that tend to be systematically marginalized within societies. Governance structures must encourage participation in deliberative and decision-making processes in order to encourage the impartial treatment of issues and to avoid the generation of structural inequalities or distortions in the allocation of resources.

(c) Effective Institutions (Impartial, Transparent, and Accountable)
Effective institutions are also crucial for good governance. This suggests not only excellent administrative capacities, but also freedom from corporate influence. As mentioned earlier, the role of money in politics in some of the oldest democracies is compromising what would otherwise be highly effective governance capacities. Both electoral results and policy outcomes can be distorted by the influence of

money in politics. This can lead to unwise and perhaps even unjust domestic- and foreign-policy decisions. A true meritocracy should be promoted, rather than a "dollarocracy."

Good governance requires the most prudent use of resources that collectively belong to the people. It therefore implies avoiding waste and eliminating corruption and inefficiencies that negatively affect the allocation of resources to serve the needs and respond to the demands of the people. Thus, another criterion of good governance is accountability. People must have the possibility and recourse to means of holding their governments accountable for the way in which resources are allocated. Accountability, however, goes beyond being responsible in using resources. It also implies taking responsibility for government actions. Yet, people cannot hold their governments accountable without access to reliable and timely information about government activities. Transparency, therefore, goes hand-in-hand with accountability and should be energetically encouraged in order to avoid conflicts of interest and the buying of influence.

3. Good Regional Governance

Regional integration has been a steady development in world politics, particularly notable in the case of the construction of the EU, the North American Free Trade Agreement (NAFTA), and the Asia-Pacific Economic Cooperation (APEC). In Europe, the regional governance structure is perhaps the most elaborate, in part due to the fact that the EU has been in existence in one form or another for several decades, whereas regional groupings in the Americas and the Asia-Pacific region are more recent developments.[238] The proliferation of regional groupings suggests, as Held notes, that *de facto* political power is no longer just located at the state level.[239] Structures of authority exist that impact institution-building at the national level, as well as norms and cognitive structures.

Given the overlapping nature of authority structures within the wider global context, it is necessary that state governance be complemented by good regional governance. The governance structures in each regional formation, however, vary in scope and form. In some regional groupings, governance structures are in place to help states coordinate their economic policies alone. In others, they influence a wider range of policy areas, including those that have traditionally been viewed as central to state sovereignty. Within the EU, for instance, governance structures in the areas of internal and external security are in place to help states coordinate in these areas. In some regions, governance structures include parliamentary assemblies, notably those within the EU. Where they do not yet exist, they should be created to increase representation at the regional level and ensure greater accountability and credibility.

Thus, when considering good governance, we have to take into account governance at the regional level, as well as at the national level. Where regional governance structures exist, they should be improved. Within the EU, for instance, a greater degree of transparency and accountability could be achieved. Where they do not yet exist, they should be created[240] so that, in instances where states cannot adequately deal with policy challenges at the national level, regional governance structures can step in to fill the vacuum.

Regional governance structures can enhance good governance through the establishment of incentives, good practices, formal systems of regulation, and monitoring mechanisms. Regional integration can also play an important role in encouraging the development of good governance through legislation, the establishment of best practices, and socialization. The EU, for example, has promoted stability and security in Eastern and Southeastern Europe, and the Mediterranean region. It has done so by expanding its membership according to good-governance criteria, as well as by promoting good-governance norms linked to human-rights standards, regional cooperation, and rule-based interaction.[241]

4. Good Global Governance

(a) Cosmopolitan International Law

Belonging to a cosmopolitan global community implies a moral commitment to those who are not fellow nationals, and this kind of commitment has to be embedded in new forms of global governance.[242] This is not to say that this commitment is not perceptible in some form at present. Cosmopolitan principles, such as egalitarian individualism, mutual recognition, consent, inclusivity, and subsidiarity, have found expression in post-World War II legal and institutional initiatives. The codification of human rights, which recognize the individual as a moral unit, came about with the creation of the UN. The UN's 1948 Universal Declaration of Human Rights and the 1966 International Covenant on Civil and Political Rights endorsed the notion that each person should be treated with equal concern and respect, regardless of the state in which they reside. Similarly, the preamble to the UN Declaration refers to people as persons with "equal and inalienable rights" and as "the foundation of freedom, justice and peace in the world."

Some have suggested that the emergence of a moral consensus about human rights was linked to the revulsion at the enormity of the crimes of the Holocaust, this being especially clear in the Declaration of Human Rights and the UN conventions against genocide and the enumeration of crimes against humanity.[243] In addition to the emergent moral consensus inspired by concern for the plight of fellow human beings, others suggest that the forces of globalization may be influencing our sense of belonging to a single "community of fate." Monique Castillo suggests, for example, that the increased intensity of transnational threats in contemporary times has contributed to the cosmopolitan condition. Transnational challenges to security, such as environmental degradation, for example, cut across national boundaries, making it increasingly harder for states to govern effectively unless they seek to cooperate with other states on a whole range of issues that were once considered the sole preserve of the nation-state. With the conceptualization and recognition of threats on a cosmopolitan scale, a shared space of responsibility and agency bridging all national frontiers is thought to be created that can (though need not) facilitate political action among people who are not co-nationals in ways that resemble national politics.[244] As a consequence, the community of fate that governs itself is no longer necessarily the political unit of the state.[245]

While cosmopolitan aspects of international law and regulation do exist, it hardly needs to be pointed out that cosmopolitan values do not always inform the actions of states. Its tremendous contribution to peace and security notwithstanding, the UN is subject to the geopolitical agendas of the most powerful states, suffers from weak enforcement mechanisms, and is not funded in the same way that it would be if states lived up to the cosmopolitan ideals of the UN Charter.[246] Narrow definitions of national interest thus continue to exist alongside the nascent cosmopolitan condition.

Cosmopolitan law should also be extended to the corporate and financial spheres. There are several reasons for this. First, economic and technological dimensions of globalization need to be regulated to minimize the space in which criminal activities can flourish.

Vladimir Petrovsky suggests that the activities of transnational companies should be regulated by a new branch of international law.[247]

(b) Effective Multilateralism
While the state is still relevant, it constitutes but one layer of governance. Good global governance requires institutional capacities and mechanisms that can complement those of states, as well as regions. Cosmopolitan global governance should be vested with an effective and accountable administrative, legislative, and executive capacity at the global level to supplement those at the national and regional levels. Where lower levels of authority structures cannot adequately manage transnational policy challenges, effective multilateralism will be required. Cosmopolitan global governance would be vested with an effective and accountable administrative, legislative, and executive capacity at the global level to supplement those at the national and regional levels. In institutional terms, this would mean, for example, reforming the UN General Assembly to make it more authoritative. Held suggests that a reformed General Assembly or something to complement it would deal with the implementation of cosmopolitan principles in, for example, the areas of health, food security, the debt burden of developing countries, global warming, and weapons proliferation. The instruments of such an assembly would need to be underpinned by a body of law specifying the core concerns of cosmopolitanism.[248]

Deliberative assemblies at the global level would be accompanied by a cosmopolitan law-enforcement and coercive capability to back up serious challenges to cosmopolitan values, entrenched in a body of cosmopolitan law.[249] While military intervention justified on the basis of national interest is less and less acceptable and intervention has increasingly to be justified according to cosmopolitan values, humanitarian or cosmopolitan interventions have often been compromised both by geopolitical interests and the unwillingness of governments to sacrifice soldiers' lives for those of strangers. A cosmopolitan crisis-management capacity would ideally be protected as much as possible from statist and power politics and placed under the auspices of representative international institutions, such as a reformed UN. A cosmopolitan force would be expected to act in order to protect people within the global community, since cosmopolitanism holds that all people belong to a single moral community before they belong to a state. A cosmopolitan crisis-management force would be multipurpose, as well as multicultural.[250]

It would also imply ensuring that multilateral institutions are not dominated by the most powerful states. These institutions ought not simply to be more representative; they should also be more transparent and accountable. The World Trade Organization (WTO), International Monetary Fund (IMF), and the World Bank should be opened up to public scrutiny and agenda-setting. The capacities of these institutions need to be accompanied by efforts to reinforce those institutions that are presently dealing with issues that are vital to augmenting social justice within a global economy. There may even be a need to establish new global governance structures that concentrate on reducing poverty, enhancing welfare, and off-setting political influence of more market-oriented agencies, such as the WTO, the IMF, and the World Bank.[251]

(c) Economic Cosmopolitanism
Many people die in the global South from preventable diseases that have been eradicated in affluent parts of the world. However, such inequalities are not confined to health but are attendant in almost every global development index. In addition to the absolute gap between developed and developing countries created as a result of two hundred years' difference in industrialization, globalizing economic trends do not reduce poverty everywhere. While there is no agreement as to whether globalization is the cause of increased global inequality, there is a general consensus that the absolute gap between the world's richest and poorest states is now at historic levels and growing.[252] The global economy, which is, at least for the time being American-centered, is a hierarchical system and, as a result, there are huge disparities of power and resources in the global political economy.[253]

Increasing inequality not only contributes to the degree of human misery, but it also influences the conditions for global stability and order. The unevenness of globalization is arguably contributing to the fragmentation of the world into zones of wealth and poverty, inclusion and exclusion, empowerment and disempowerment. This contributes to increased incidents of failed states, feelings of alienation, perceived injustice, transnational terrorism, the spread of weapons of mass destruction, transnational organized crime, as well as ethnic conflicts. According to Anthony McGrew in his article "Cosmopolitanism and Global Justice," a cosmopolitan order needs to promote greater justice, help to heal past injustices that continue to contaminate the present, and to empower the most vulnerable.[254]

A global economy informed by cosmopolitan values would take measures to improve the market access of developing countries. While many developing countries have become more open economically, developed countries still maintain forms of protectionism. Average tariff rates may be low in developed countries, but tariffs remain in areas where developing countries enjoy a comparative advantage, such as agriculture and labor-intensive manufactures. Based on 2002 calculations, protectionism in developed countries is causing developing countries to lose up to $100 billion a year. To put this in perspective, this is equivalent to twice the amount of foreign development aid from the global North to the global South.[255] A global economy informed by cosmopolitanism would encourage trade liberalization that focuses on market access for developing countries in areas where they have a comparative advantage.

(d) Coexistence of Civilizations (Mutual Awareness, Recognition, Respect, and Exchanges)

Against the backdrop of intensified migration, irregular immigration, xenophobic and exclusionary tendencies in host societies with regard to race, political beliefs, and religion, as well as radical transformations occurring within some societies, the peaceful coexistence of civilizations is critical to dealing effectively with the multitude of challenges facing states, ranging from demographic changes to international terrorism.

Culture, which provides the scaffolding for civilizational forms, is not static. Large collective identities typically become securitized because their holders feel threatened as a consequence of change. Globalization is likely to increase the extent to which members of different cultural groups come into contact with one another. Moreover, non-Western societies have to adapt to a Western-, and in particular US-, dominated global system. As internal dynamics interact with changes in the global environment, they may produce cultural turmoil.

The starting point for international cultural dialogue, as Dieter Senghaas suggests, should be the differentiation processes that are currently unfolding within traditional cultures across the world. In particular, it is important to be aware of the disarray that changes in the broader global environment may be causing.[256] We also need to find ways of spreading knowledge that might serve to nurture coexistence among people and groups in a globalizing world. Increasing awareness about one another is a prerequisite for mutual recognition and respect. Inter-civilizational exchanges need to be seen as a source of stimulation and dynamism. Indeed, civilizations that aspire to play a critical role in today's world cannot avoid interdependence.

5. Conclusion

In this chapter, we discussed the importance of good governance (domestic, regional, and global) for global security. At the domestic level, we argued that good governance involves the protection of basic civil and human rights, inclusivity (socioeconomic, cultural, and political), and effective institutions (impartial, transparent, and accountable). Good global governance, however, entails overlapping structures of authority. States, while still relevant, do not constitute the only locus of authority. Governance structures at the regional level, where they already exist, should be participatory, transparent, and accountable, taking on transnational questions that cannot be dealt with adequately at the state level. Where they do not yet exist, they should be established. At the global level, good governance implies the primacy of cosmopolitan law, effective multilateralism and multilateral bodies, economic cosmopolitanism, and the promotion of ways of increasing peaceful co-existence and exchanges between civilizations.

CHAPTER 7

CONCLUSION

At the outset of this book, we explained that security has undergone a process of reconceptualization during the course of the last decade and a half. The traditional approach to security that dominated both the discipline of IR, as well as state practice, was concerned above all with the security of the state and the accumulation of military power as a means to achieve this end. Attempts to disturb this comfortable yet simplistic formulation got under way in earnest following the end of the Cold War. The effort to provide a more adequate framework for analysis and guide for policy makers has taken a variety of shapes. Some scholars have underscored the possibility of overcoming the constraints of international anarchy through collective security arrangements. Others have argued in favor of broadening the scope of Security Studies to include non-military issues, such as the environment, migration, and organized crime, as well as the more traditional military threats to security. Others went still further, proposing that the individual rather than the state should be the primary object that should be secured. This took the form of a human-security paradigm, which developed as much as a result of emerging state practice as academic reformulation. Efforts to combine elements of all of the above have also appeared under the rubric of cooperative security.

In Chapter 2, we reviewed these attempts to reformulate security. To reiterate, proponents of collective security, it was argued, called into question the realist assumption that institutions do not have a significant role to play in enhancing security and stability. While the concept of collective security accepts that military force continues to play a central role in international life, it contends that there are ways to escape the security dilemma, in which one state's security is another state's insecurity. Collective security requires states not only to renounce the use of force to alter the international status quo and to resolve their disputes peaceably. It also implies that states take into account the broader good when formulating their national interest.

Insofar as it has helped to dampen security competition between states, collective security has made a tremendous contribution to international relations, most notably in the present-day form of the UN. The value of collective security as a practice not withstanding, the concept, nevertheless, did not depart fundamentally from the focus on the state and the use of military force that characterizes the traditional security paradigm. As such, recourse to it alone is insufficient to address the multifarious contemporary security challenges. The need to shift the focus from the state and the military was made clear by the increased visibility of intrastate conflict, particularly within the context of the collapse of the Soviet Union and the former Yugoslavia. In addition, a number of other issues that were previously not considered security concerns became securitized (i.e., raised to the level of security rather than political or criminal issues).

In response to these concerns, an effort to include non-military issues within the scope of Security Studies got under way. Despite a fierce debate within the field about the desirability of broadening the security agenda, most people now recognize security as involving more than deterrence and the use of military force. Other issues, such as the trafficking of drugs and human beings, now form part of the security repertoire of policy makers, as well as academics. Moreover, the functions of military alliances are undergoing a process of transformation, and states are now equally concerned with police and border cooperation and capacity-building within fragile states as they are with military threats.

Against this backdrop, some of the Copenhagen School's most prominent figures (Buzan, Waever, and de Wilde) proposed a classification of security into sectors: military, political, economic, environmental, and societal. This approach allowed for referent objects of security other than the state. Indeed, one of the most innovative aspects of this approach was the identification of large-scale collective identities as something to be secured. Moreover, the fact that collective identities were recognized as functioning independently of the state meant that the assumption that if the state was secure then the citizenry would be also be secure was being called into question. Despite these contributions, the societal approach failed to break entirely with the state-centrism of the realist security paradigm.

A more definitive break with state-centrism came with the emergence of the human-security paradigm, which had as its objective the deepening of security. It is perceived by its proponents as more comprehensive than efforts to broaden the scope of security. Some states, such as Canada and Norway, even argue that human security, broadly defined as freedom from want and fear, should form a central part of foreign policy. These developments are very positive, since national security is no longer simply national but also transnational, involving non-military threats and non-state actors, and, moreover, it affects civilians as much as combatants.

In some formulations, all of these dimensions have found expression in the concept of cooperative security. This concept implies more than collective security since states are expected to cooperate in areas that go well beyond deterrence and the use of force. Indeed, many contemporary security challenges require police and intelligence cooperation, for example, both of which have traditionally been fundamental facets of state sovereignty. Like collective security, it also recognizes that states must not only cooperate, but that lasting cooperation is possible despite the condition of international anarchy. Yet, in the cooperative-security approach, states cooperate in response to transnational security challenges that are usually non-military in nature and often require non-military responses. It also goes beyond collective security in that it recognizes that the situation in neighboring areas is also a vital component of security within a cooperative-security zone. Moreover, advancing security within this framework begins with human security, upon which all other security depends.

To a great extent, the cooperative-security approach informs a great deal of state practice. The pursuit of security and stability is widely understood as involving more than the accumulation of military power. Most policy makers and academics regularly espouse the virtues of transnational cooperation and institution-building within transition states, for example. Moreover, as mentioned, some states have already made human security a central pillar of their foreign policy. Yet, one dimension of security that merits greater attention, especially at this point in time, is the issue of transcultural relations. In our view, security is not only no longer national but is transnational in its dimensions; it is also transcultural in the sense that relations between diverse cultures are vital to global security. While the attacks in New York and Washington in 2001, in Madrid in 2004, and in London in 2005, civil unrest in France in 2005, and the reactions to the Mohammed cartoons published in a Danish newspaper[257] have all served to highlight the desperate need for greater transcultural security, this particular element of security has yet to be given sufficient and deliberate attention by the approaches to security, even by those that take a self-consciously comprehensive approach to security.

In many respects, the field of Security Studies has come a long way since the early days of the post-Cold War period. We are now better equipped analytically, as well as practically, to respond to the multitude of security challenges faced today, even though we still have a long way to go. At least ethnic conflict, human trafficking, and security-sector reform, for example, are on the security agendas of many states and receive the attention of international organizations and non-governmental organizations. The same cannot be said for transcultural tensions. Transcultural issues are only just beginning to be elevated to the level of security issues in large part because the consequences of neglecting them are only now being painfully felt in the West.

This book set out to propose a more comprehensive approach to security that is capable of capturing a multitude of security challenges and allowing for different referent objects of security. Doing so required us to delineate a classification of global security that allowed for a number of referent objects of security to be considered. To some extent it builds on, but attempts to go beyond Buzan, Waever, and de Wilde's sectoral approach. Specifically, we suggested that global security may be thought of analytically as comprising five substrates: **human, environmental, national, transnational, and transcultural.**

The first substrate, human security, refers to the security of individuals. The second, environmental security, refers to the security of the biosphere. The third substrate, national security, refers to the state's population, economic situation, and organizational integrity. The fourth substrate that we identified was transnational security, which indicates globalization-mediated security of states against transnational threats. The fifth is transcultural security, which refers to ensuring that a plurality of cultures and civilizations can coexist without their relations being elevated to security issues.

Our objective in classifying global security in this way was to provide a framework that was capable of identifying the diverse array of phenomena that impact individual, state, and cultural security. While the sectoral approach, the human-security paradigm, and cooperative security together allow for each of these referents to be treated as objects of security, no one approach gives adequate attention to the individual, the state, and culture. In particular, our classification aimed to bring the issue of transcultural relations, traditionally marginalized by realism, to center stage, something that Buzan, Waever, and de Wilde started to do in their specification of a societal-security sector. Indeed, the notion of societal security was perhaps the most important contribution the sectoral approach made to the study of security. It has immediate relevance in the context of increased migration and defensive reactions on the part of more established "host" societies. The notion of societal security is able to capture this in that it acknowledges that large-scale collective identities may not be coterminous with the state, potentially making them objects of security in their own right. Whether this is the case or not would depend on how collective identities evolve in relation to other developments. They are most likely to be perceived to be under threat in relation to issues such as migration, friction with a neighboring culture, or an integration project, for example.

With our fifth substrate of global security, transcultural security, we identify cultures and civilizational forms as referent objects. Earlier, we defined culture as a refined awareness of the religious tradition, customs, and the institutional and aesthetic achievements of a nation or group. It is the scaffolding on which civilizations, which refers to advanced systems of social organization, are built. Allowing for both culture, experienced at the individual and group level, and civilization, understood as a form of social organization, to be considered as potential objects of security helps to capture the sense in which cultural issues can become security concerns at the sub-national as well as supranational level. In our view, cultures and civilizations need to evolve in relation to developments in a non-exclusive manner in order to assure transcultural security. While competition can occasionally generate improvements in the human condition, synergistic relations need to be developed between the diverse cultural groups and civilizational forms. At the level of the international political community, alliance-building and the coexistence of civilizations are paramount to effectively addressing security challenges. The notion of transcultural security is vital today, since people from different cultures and systems of social organization are less isolated than they were in the Middle Ages, for example. It is clear that intensified interaction will generate mixed reactions. Therefore, it will fall upon us to promote confidence among people and groups with differing cultural heritages, as well as between different (yet related) civilizations. When acting together, people identifying with different cultures and civilizational forms can have a greater impact on global security than they would have individually. This, we suggest, might be thought of as synergy, implying mutual coexistence, between cultures and civilizations. This we termed transcultural synergy. This is the end to which transcultural security should aspire.

The five dimensions of global security, as we called them, were then discussed in greater detail in Chapter 3. Specifically, we defined our understanding of each substrate of global security. We then discussed some of the most prevalent issues within each security domain, as well as briefly reviewed achievements in this substrate and remaining challenges.

We explained that the first of the substrates, human security, was initially defined as a concept and employed within the context of the UN system. In broad terms, it refers to freedom from fear and from want. This implies the eradication of hunger and illness, respect for human rights and dignity, as well as the absence of violence and armed conflict that, for the most part, affects civilians. The dimensions of human security can be further broken down into economic, food, health, environmental, personal, community, and political security. With a focus on the individual, human security helps to reveal the interconnection between diverse security concerns. A conflict may involve, for example, the use of small arms or the use of child soldiers, and it may be partly funded with gains from drug trafficking. Many human insecurities have been intensified as the processes of globalization have helped generate the emergence of new threats and intensification of many old threats. Some of the most prominent human-security threats stem from human trafficking, health risks, global organized crime, financial- and labor-market instabilities, poverty, conflict, and development.

While focusing on human security helps to highlight complex relationships between a number of phenomena and the need to address them in parallel, the practice of human security remains difficult and uneven. States face the difficulty of adapting policy frameworks and systems of social protection to rapidly unfolding developments. At the global level, the challenge is to recognize the interrelated nature of numerous security challenges and to devise comprehensive security strategies. Adopting a human-security approach offers a better chance of effectively promoting greater security and stability.

The second substrate of classification of security is environmental security. We explained that, while the environment has traditionally been associated with conservation and development, global climate change, in particular, has resulted in the environment being seen as a security issue. The implications of global environmental change have been considered in a variety of ways. Many interpretations have focused on its impact on national security. Others have emphasized its impact on individual security. Environmental security may also be understood as referring to the physical and biological facets of the natural world. Whether our concern with the environment should result in the biosphere itself or the maintenance of a certain level of civilization becoming the referent of security is contested. We argued that both may serve as referent objects of environmental security, depending on the specific problem at hand.

Responsiveness to environmental-security concerns has been variable. Leading actors tend to be active in relation to particular issues. These actors are sometimes states. However, they often face the difficulty of responding to environmental-security issues and competing interests at the domestic level. In addition, some environmental-security problems are linked to inadequate governance within states. At the global level, efforts to enhance environmental security encounter a number of difficulties: The benefits are enjoyed by a multitude, while the costs are primarily born by a few, primarily those in the private sector; multilateral initiatives are also complicated by the North-South dimension; and the scientific evidence linking global environmental change with human activities is contested. Thus, there remains much to be done.

Our third substrate of global security was identified as national security, which we subdivided into military, political, economic, and societal dimensions. States have, of course, constituted the primary referent object of security, and, due to the traditional organizing concept of the state system, securing the state has been intimately tied with the use of force. Externally, this has been represented in dominant understandings of national security through the accumulation of military and sometimes economic means. However, because IR has rested on a rigid domestic-international dichotomy, the internal aspects of national security have been marginalized in the realist paradigm. For this reason, we have included political and societal security in our definition of national security. Political security refers to the stability of institutionalized authority within a state. Perceptions of threats to political security typically emanate from challenges to traditional notions of sovereignty. They may originate internally, in the form of challenges to the ideological legitimacy of the state, or externally, in the form of a denial of the recognition of sovereignty. Societal security is understood as the protection of the state population, which may not always carry an identity.

The fourth substrate that we identified was transnational security, which involves globalization-mediated security of states against transnational threats that include any kind of illegal cross-border movements, such as human and drug trafficking, irregular migration, and environmental degradation. What is typically at threat is the social, economic, and political integrity of the state or the quality of life of its inhabitants. One of the difficulties posed by transnational threats is their emergence over long and indefinite periods of time. In addition, the global social, economic, and political challenges that have emerged as a result of the forces of globalization and the collapse of communism have intensified many of these transnational types of threats.

The fifth element in our classification of global security is transcultural security, which refers to the integrity of diverse cultural groups and civilizational forms. We were motivated to include transcultural security by the marginalization of culture by the traditional security paradigm. We took our cue from the Copenhagen School's innovative concept of societal security, which contributed to the identification of cultural issues as security concerns and, specifically, the recognition that collective identities exist that are not always coterminous with the state. In our view, ensuring the integrity of the cultural heritage of individuals and groups, as well as civilizations, is vital to enhancing security and stability. At the transnational level, coexistence between civilizations will be central to dealing effectively with transnational threats to security. This is especially the case in the context of intensified transcultural interaction. Yet, there needs not only to be coexistence between large-scale collective identities, but a synergy between different cultural identities and civilizations. We argued that a plurality of cultures and civilizational forms can have a net effect on global security that is greater than would be the case in the event of isolated responses. Transcultural security is imperative to creating the conditions under which this may be possible.

While these five dimensions of security were analytically separated, they are interrelated in reality. Identifying the separate substrata of global security helps to discern multiple and interlinked aspects of insecurity. This contributes to a more comprehensive view of the challenges we face in terms of security and demonstrates the need to address multiple facets of security simultaneously given the complementarity between each of the five dimensions.

Having set out our classification of global security, we then explored the linkage between injustice and insecurity. We defined justice as referring in general terms to the morally correct distribution of benefits and burdens. Since justice is a nuanced concept with various meanings, what it entails will depend on the specifics of the issue at hand. We then looked at the relationship between injustice, alienation, frustration, and anger, potentially leading to extreme forms of action.

While it may seem self-evident that injustice, whether perceived or real, can lead to insecurity of various kinds, it is rarely identified as a specific security issue. Sentiments of injustice, if left unaddressed can, however, generate mistrust, animosity, and alienation, among other things. Understanding the origins of perceptions of injustice, where they exist, are, therefore, important if we are to successfully prevent conflicts from emerging or reconstruct war-torn societies, for instance.

In Chapter 5, we proposed a new security principle called the multi-sum security principle. This combines our proposed classification of global security, which comprises five aspects of security – human, environmental, national, transnational, and transcultural security – and the conviction that justice is a prerequisite for security. Specifically, the multi-sum security principle states that: **"In a globalized world, security can no longer be thought of as a zero-sum game involving states alone. Global security, instead, has five dimensions that include human, environmental, national, transnational, and transcultural security, and, therefore, global security and the security of any state or culture cannot be achieved without good governance at all levels that guarantees security through *justice* for *all* individuals, states, and cultures."**

Given the importance of good governance to the administration of justice, in Chapter 6, we argued that good governance is an essential medium for enhancing justice and, thus, security, in developing countries, countries in transition from communism, and mature democracies that are failing to deliver in this area. We proposed that good governance involves overlapping authority structures and public-policy frameworks at the local, state, regional, and wider global levels, based on the principles of subsidiarity, inclusivity, openness, and accountability, backed up by cosmopolitan international law.

In sum, this book has attempted to do three things. First, it proposed a classification of global security, consisting of five interrelated substrata, which constitutes an attempt to provide a comprehensive framework with which to examine challenges and generate responses to security concerns. While human, environmental, national, transnational, and transcultural security are analytically separated, they are interlinked and complementary. Separating them out helps to identify the specific facets of particular security issues.

Second, it argued that injustice should be conceived as a security concern, given that it can lead to emotions such as frustration and anger, which risk generating a breakdown of communication and extreme forms of behavior. Lastly, it maintained that ensuring that injustice is avoided or addressed wherever its appears requires good governance at all levels.

REFERENCES

[1] United Nations Development Programme, *International Cooperation at the Crossroads: Aid, Trade and Security in an Unequal World*, Human Development Report 2005 (New York: UNDP, 2005).

[2] "Patterns of Major Armed Conflicts," http://www.sipri.org/contents/conflict/MAC_patterns.html.

[3] United Nations Development Programme, *op. cit.*, note 1.

[4] G. Burnham, R. Lafta, S. Doocy, and L. Roberts, "Mortality before and after the 2003 invasion of Iraq: A Cross-sectional Cluster Sample Survey," *The Lancet*, October 11, 2006.

[5] See Table 44 in C. Langton, *The Military Balance 2006* (London: Routledge for the IISS, 2006), pp. 398-403.

[6] This lower-end estimate is based on the cost of operations in Iraq alone. Higher-end estimates would also include the cost of diplomatic operations, foreign aid to Iraq, medical expenses of veterans, and pensions to those families that have suffered fatalities. J. Weisman, "Projected Costs of War Soar," *The Washington Post*, April 27, 2006, p. A16.

[7] "International Criminal Accountability and Children's Rights," United Nations University Policy Brief No. 2, 2006, p. 1.

[8] United Nations Development Programme, *op. cit.*, note 1.

[9] "The Millennium Development Goals Report 2006," United Nations Department of Economic and Social Affairs, New York, June 2006, p. 6.

[10] J.H. Herz, "Idealist Internationalism and the Security Dilemma," *World Politics*, Vol. 2, Issue 2, January 1950, pp. 157-158.

[11] S. Walt, "The Renaissance of Security Studies," *International Studies Quarterly*, Vol. 35, Issue 2, 1991, pp. 211-239; E.A. Kolodziej, "Renaissance of Security Studies? Caveat Lector!" *International Studies Quarterly*, Vol. 36, Issue 4, 1992, pp. 421-438; S. Dalby, "Contesting an Essential Concept: Reading the Dilemmas in Contemporary Security Discourse," in K. Krause and M.C. Williams (eds.) *Critical Security Studies: Concepts and Cases* (Minneapolis: University of Minnesota Press, 1997).

[12] B. Buzan, O. Waever, and J. de Wilde, *Security: A New Framework for Analysis* (Boulder, CO, London: Lynne Rienner, 1998), pp. 195-197.

[13] See R. Cohen and M. Mihalka, "Cooperative Security: New Horizons for International Order," The Marshall Center Papers, No. 3, April 2001.

[14] P.R. Viotti and M.V. Kauppi, *International Relations Theory: Realism, Pluralism, Globalism, and Beyond*, (Boston: Allyn and Bacon, 1999), 3rd edition, pp. 6-7; 64-65.

[15] R. Gilpin, with the assistance of J.M. Gilpin, *The Political Economy of International Relations* (Princeton, New Jersey: Princeton University Press, 1987).

[16] See H. Morgenthau, *Politics Among Nations, The Struggle for Power and Peace* (New York: Alfred A. Knopf, 1948),

[17] T. Dunne, "Realism," in J. Baylis and S. Smith (eds.) *The Globalization of World Politics: An Introduction to International Relations* (Oxford: Oxford University Press, 1999), p. 113.

[18] Herz, *op. cit.*, note 10.

[19] See K.N. Waltz, *Theory of International Politics* (Reading, Mass.: Addison-Wesley, 1979).

[20] R.J. Art and R. Jervis, *International Politics: Enduring Concepts and Contemporary Issues* (New York: Longman, 2003), Ch. 1.
[21] Dunne, *op. cit.*, note 17, p. 115.
[22] J. Donnelly, *Realism and International Relations* (Cambridge: Cambridge University Press, 2000), p. 9.
[23] E.H. Carr, *The Twenty Years' Crisis, 1919-1939: An Introduction to the Study of International Relations* (London: Macmillan, 1946), p. 89.
[24] Dunne, *op. cit.*, note 17, pp. 117-118.
[25] H. Suganami, "British Institutionalists, or the English School, 20 Years On," *International Relations*, Vol. 17, No. 3, September 2003, p. 257.
[26] See Cohen and Mihalka, *op. cit.*, note 13.
[27] *Ibid.*, p. 6.
[28] G. Evans, "Cooperative Security and Intrastate Conflict," *Foreign Policy*, No. 96, Fall 1994, pp. 1-2.
[29] See B. Buzan, *People, States and Fear: National Security Problem in International Relations* (Chapel Hill: University of North Carolina Press, 1983).
[30] See O. Waever, "Securitization and Desecuritization," in R.D. Lipschutz (ed.) *On Security* (New York: Columbia University Press, 1998).
[31] Buzan *et al.*, *op. cit.*, note 12, p. 7.
[32] *Ibid.*, pp. 22-24 and 195-197.
[33] P. Hough, *Understanding Global Security* (London and New York: Routledge, 2004), p. 9.
[34] United Nations Development Programme, *New Dimensions of Human Security*, Human Development Report 1994 (New York: UNDP, 1994).
[35] K. Derghoukassian, "Human Security: A Brief Report of the State of the Art," The Dante B. Fascell North-South Center, Working Paper No. 3, November 2001, pp. 2-3.
[36] Evans, *op. cit.*, note 28, p. 2.
[37] Cohen and Mihalka, *op. cit.*, note 13, pp. 7-9.
[38] Buzan *et al.*, *op. cit.*, note 12, p. 119.
[39] *Ibid.*, pp. 23, 121.
[40] J.C. Kapur, "Transcending the Clash of Civilizations," *World Affairs*, Vol. 7, No. 2, April-June 2003, http://www.ciaonet.org/olj/wa/wa_apr03_a.html.
[41] S. Alkire, "Concepts of Human Security," in L. Chen, S. Fukuda-Parr, and E. Seidensticker (eds.) *Human Insecurity in a Global World* (Cambridge, Mass.: Harvard University Press, 2003), p. 15.
[42] A. Betts and M. Eagleton-Pierce, "Editorial Introduction: 'Human Security'," *STAIR*, Vol. 1, No. 2, 2005, p. 5.
[43] M. Fell, "Is Human Security Our Main Concern in the 21st Century?" *Journal of Security Sector Management*, Vol. 4, No. 3, 2006, pp. 1-2.
[44] *Ibid.*
[45] Hough, *op. cit.*, note 33, p. 9.
[46] *Ibid.*, p. 13.
[47] United Nations Development Programme, *op. cit.*, note 34.
[48] *Ibid.*, p. 15-16.
[49] D. Henk, "Human Security: Relevance and Implications," *Parameters*, Vol. 35, No. 4, 2005, p. 1.
[50] Hough, *op. cit.*, note 33, p. 14.

⁵¹ See the Human Security Network's Website at: http://www.humansecuritynetwork.org/.
⁵² Fell, *op. cit.*, note 43, p. 5.
⁵³ Henk, *op. cit.*, note 49.
⁵⁴ Fell, *op. cit.*, note 43, p. 5.
⁵⁵ R. McRae, "Human Security in a Globalized World," in. R. McRae and. D,. Hubert (eds.) *Human Security and the New Diplomacy: Protecting People, Promoting Peace* (Montreal: McGill-Queen's University Press, 2001), p. 21.
⁵⁶ S. Fukuda-Parr, "New Threats to Human Security in the Era of Globalization," in Chen, Fukuda-Parr, and Seidensticker *op. cit.*, note 41, p. 4.
⁵⁷ R.L. Bach, "Global Mobility, Inequality and Security," in Chen *et al.*, *ibid.*, p. 67.
⁵⁸ *Ibid.*, pp. 67-68.
⁵⁹ A. Nichols Pratt, "Human Trafficking: the Nadir of an Unholy Trinity," in A. Aldis and G.P. Herd, *Soft Security Threats and European Security* (London and New York: Routledge, 2005), pp. 65; 69-70.
⁶⁰ *Ibid.*, pp. 7-8.
⁶¹ L. Chen and V. Narasimham, "Global Health and Human Security," Chen *et al.*, *op. cit.*, note 41, pp. 185-186.
⁶² C. Watts, "Domestic Violence: Violation of Women's Rights by their Intimate Partners," in M. Vlachova and L. Biason, *Women in an Insecure World* (Geneva: Geneva Centre for the Democratic Control of Armed Forces, 2005), p. 55.
⁶³ Chen and Narasimham, *op. cit.*, note 61, pp. 188-190.
⁶⁴ *Ibid.*, pp. 6-7.
⁶⁵ Fell, *op. cit.*, note 43, pp. 6-7.
⁶⁶ Hough, *op. cit.*, note 33, pp. 219-220.
⁶⁷ S. Griffith-Jones and J. Kimmis, "Human Insecurity of International Financial Volatility," in Chen *et al.*, *op. cit.*, note 41, p. 163.
⁶⁸ *Ibid.,* pp. 163-164, 166.
⁶⁹ *Ibid.*, pp. 8-9.
⁷⁰ *Ibid.*, pp. 164, 167-8.
⁷¹ Griffith-Jones and Kimmis, *op. cit.*, note 67, pp. 171-172.
⁷² *Ibid.*, p. 9.
⁷³ "Poverty, Infectious Disease, and Environmental Degradation as Threats to Collective Security: A UN Panel Report," *Population and Development Review*, Vol. 31, No. 3, 2005.
⁷⁴ C. Lindsey, "Vulnerability of Women," in Vlachova and Biason, *op. cit.* note 62, p. 109; C. Lindsey, "Rape and Other Forms of Sexual Violence," in Vlachova and Biason, *op. cit.*, note 62, p. 113.
⁷⁵ C. Sorger and E. Hoskins, "Protecting the Most Vulnerable: War-Affected Children," in McRae and Hubert, *op. cit.*, note 55, p. 136.
⁷⁶ S. Hanson, "Case Study: Bosnia and Herzegovina," in McRae and Hubert, *ibid.*, p. 94.
⁷⁷ L. Axworthy, "Introduction," in *op. cit.*, note 55, p. 6.
⁷⁸ Fukuda-Parr, *op. cit.*, note 56, p. 10.
⁷⁹ Axworthy, *op. cit.*, note 77.
⁸⁰ *Ibid.*, p. 8.
⁸¹ *Ibid.*, pp. 11-12.

[82] *Ibid.*, pp. 11-12.
[83] N.R.F. Al-Rodhan, "Editorial of Policy Brief on Changing Health Paradigms, Globalization, and Global Security," in N.R.F. Al-Rodhan (ed.) *Policy Briefs on the Transnational Aspects of Security and Stability* (Berlin and Zürich: LIT, 2007), p. 182.
[84] E. Munro, "Natural Disasters, Globalization, and the Implications for Global Security," in Al-Rodhan, *ibid.*, p. 182.
[85] S. Hargreaves, "Senator Calls for Gasoline Price Fix Probe," *CNN Money*, April 18, 2006.
[86] O. Greene, "Environmental Issues," in Baylis and Smith, *op. cit.*, note 17, p. 389.
[87] See, for example, R. Falk, *This Endangered Planet* (New York: Random House, 1971).
[88] J. Barnett, "Security and Climate Change," Tyndall Centre for Climate Change Research, Working Paper, No. 7, October 2001, pp. 3-4.
[89] *Ibid.*, p. 4.
[90] K. Klubnikin and D. Causey, "Environmental Security: Metaphor for the Millennium," *Seton Hall Journal of Diplomacy and International Relations*, Vol. 3, No. 2, 2002, p. 113.
[91] *Ibid.*, p. 111.
[92] Buzan *et al.*, *op. cit.*, note 12, p. 76.
[93] *Ibid.*, p. 80.
[94] *Ibid.*, pp. 76-77.
[95] J.R. McNeil, *An Environmental History of the Twentieth-Century World: Something New Under the Sun* (New York and London: W.W. Norton & Company, 2000), pp. 3-4.
[96] *Ibid.*, pp. 6-7.
[97] *Ibid.*, pp. 8-9.
[98] *Ibid.*, p. 10.
[99] *Ibid.*, p. 15.
[100] *Ibid.*, p. 17.
[101] Buzan *et al.*, *op. cit.*, note 12, pp. 81-82.
[102] *Ibid.*, pp. 80-1.
[103] F. McNeill, "Making Sense of Environmental Security," The North-South Agenda Papers, No. 39, The Dante B. Fascell North-South Center, University of Miami, 2000, p. 1.
[104] Klubnikin and Causey, *op. cit.*, note 90, p. 117.
[105] McNeill, *op. cit.*, note 103, p. 229.
[106] Klubnikin and Causey, *op. cit.*, note 90, p. 117.
[107] *Ibid.*
[108] *Ibid.*
[109] J. Goldstein, *International Relations* (New York: Longman, 1999), pp. 471-472.
[110] H. Haftendorn, "Water and International Conflict," paper presented at the International Studies Association, 40th Annual Convention, Washington, DC, February 16-20, 1999, p.1.
[111] Goldstein, *op. cit.*, note 109, p. 491.

[112] The Economic and Development Review Committee, Organisation for Economic Co-operation and Development, *Improving Water Management: Recent OECD Experience* (Paris: OECD, February 21, 2003).
[113] *Ibid.*
[114] Goldstein, *op. cit.*, note 109, p. 492.
[115] A. Peshard-Sverdrup and M. Bishop, "U.S.-Mexico Transboundary Water Management: The Case of the Rio Grande/Rio Bravo," The Center for Strategic and International Studies, January 2003.
[116] Haftendorn, *op. cit.*, note 110.
[117] Barnett, *op. cit.*, note 88, p. 8.
[118] Goldstein, *op. cit.*, note 109, p. 471.
[119] World Meteorological Organization "Living with Climate Variation and Risk," *World Climate News*, No. 29, June 2006, p. 4.
[120] J. Lash and R. Repetto "Planetary Roulette: Gambling with the Climate," *Foreign Policy*, No. 108, Fall 1997; World Meteorological Organization, *ibid.*
[121] Hough, *op. cit.*, note 33, Ch. 8.
[122] N.R.F. Al- Rodhan, "Editorial of Policy Brief on Natural Disasters, Globalization, and the Implications for Global Security," in Al-Rodhan, *op. cit.*, note 83.
[123] Barnett, *op. cit.*, note 88, p. 7.
[124] Goldstein, *op. cit.*, note 109, p. 475.
[125] K. Civerolo, S. Gaffin, R. Goldberg, C. Hogrefe, P.L. Kinney, K. Knowlton, J. Ku, B. Lynn, and J.E. Rosenthal, C. Rosenzweig, "Assessing Ozone-Related Health Impacts under a Changing Climate," *Environmental Health Perspectives*, Vol. 112, No. 15, 2004.
[126] S. Dalby, "Security and Ecology in the Age of Globalization," in *ECSP Report*, Issue 8, Environmental Change and Security Project, Woodrow Wilson Foundation for International Scholars, 2002, p. 101.
[127] Buzan *et al.*, *op. cit.*, note 12, p. 77.
[128] J. Wallace, "US Environmental Policy and Global Security," in Al-Rodhan, *op. cit.*, note 83.
[129] *Ibid.*, p. 187.
[130] A. Najam, "The Human Dimensions of Environmental Security: Some Insights from South Asia," in ECSP Report, Issue No. 9, 2003, accessed online at: http://wwics.si.edu/topics/pubs/najam.pdf.
[131] Goldstein, *op. cit.*, note 109, pp. 472-473.
[132] See the UNFCCC website: www.unfccc.int.
[133] Goldstein, *op. cit.*, note 109, p. 475.
[134] Wallace, *op. cit.*, note 128.
[135] Buzan *et al.*, *op. cit.*, note 12, pp. 77, 79.
[136] M. Brusasco-Mackenzie, "Environmental Security: A View from Europe," in *ECSP Report*, Issue 8, Environmental Change and Security Project, Woodrow Wilson Foundation for International Scholars, 2005, p. 18.
[137] "A Secure Europe in a Better World," EU Security Strategy, Brussels, December 12, 2003, accessed at: http://ue.eu.int/uedocs/cmsUpload/78367.pdf.
[138] Brusasco-Mackenzie, *op. cit.*, note 136, pp. 15-16.
[139] Buzan *et al.*, *op. cit.*, note 12, pp. 50-51.

[140] Ibid., p. 50; O. Waever, "Securitization and Desecurization," in R.D. Lipschutz (ed.) *On Security* (New York: Columbia University Press, 1995).
[141] D. Lutterbeck, "Policing Migration in the Mediterranean," *Mediterranean Politics*, Vol. 11, No. 1, 2006, pp. 59-82.
[142] T. Tardy, "Introduction," in T. Tardy (ed.) *Peace Operations After 11 September 2001* (London and New York: Routledge, 2004), pp. 1-2; Buzan *et al.*, *op. cit.*, note 12, p. 49.
[143] B. Buzan, *People, States and Fear* (London: HarvesterWheatsheaf, 1991), pp. 141, 143.
[144] Ibid., G. Herd, "Political Security and Globalization," in N.R.F. Al-Rodhan (ed.), *The Geopolitical and Geosecurity Implications of Globalization* (Geneva: Éditions Slatkine, 2006), p. 186.
[145] Buzan, *op. cit.*, note 143.
[146] Herd, *op. cit.*, note 144, p. 188.
[147] R. Mandel, *Armies without States: The Privatization of Security* (Boulder, CO, London: Lynne Rienner, 2002), p. 8.
[148] Ibid., pp. 3-13.
[149] B. Nichiporuk, *The Security Dynamics of Demographic Factors* (Santa Monica: Rand, 2000), pp. 40, 42.
[150] Ibid., p. 43.
[151] Buzan *et al.*, *op. cit.*, note 12, p. 97.
[152] See C. Dent, *Foreign Economic Policies of Singapore, South Korea and Taiwan* (Cheltenham: Edward Elgar, 2002).
[153] Buzan *et al.*, *op. cit.*, note 12, p. 99.
[154] P. Gowan, *The Global Gamble: Washington's Faustian Bid for World Dominance* (London, New York: Verso, 1999).
[155] Buzan *et al.*, *op. cit.*, note 12, p. 98.
[156] Ibid., p. 119.
[157] Ibid.
[158] O. Waever, "Societal Security: The Concept," in O. Waever, B. Buzan, M. Kelstrup, and P. Lemaitre, *Identity, Migration and the New Security Agenda in Europe* (New York: St. Martin's Press, 1993), p. 20.
[159] International Organization for Migration, see http://www.iom.int/jahia/page254.html.
[160] See S. Djajic, "Potential Outcomes of Migration Flux in a Globalized World and Its Security Implications," in N.R.F. Al-Rodhan (ed.) *Policy Briefs on the Transcultural Aspects of Security and Stability* (Berlin and Zürich: LIT, 2006).
[161] B. Webster, "Societal Security and Globalization," in Al-Rodhan, *op. cit.*, note 144, pp. 147-148.
[162] Nichiporuk, *op. cit.*, note 149, p. 2.
[163] Ibid., p. 27.
[164] "Europe's Population Is Getting Older, How Will This Affect Us and What Should We Do About It?" *European Commission Green Paper on Demographic Change*, March 17, 2005.
[165] Nichiporuk, *op. cit.*, note 149, p. 47.
[166] J. Diamond, *Guns, Germs, and Steel* (London, New York: W.W. Norton and Company, 1997).

[167] Webster, *op. cit.*, note 161, p. 151.
[168] Merriam-Webster Online, accessed June 7, 2006, http://www.m-w.com/, s.v. "transnational."
[169] S. Chledowski, "Military Corruption and Organized Crime in Eastern Europe and the Caucasus," *Journal of Military and Strategic Studies*, Vol. 7, No. 4, 2005, p. 4.
[170] *Ibid.*, p. 8.
[171] *Ibid.*, p. 1.
[172] J.C. Ross, "Securitizing Migration after 11 March," *Area: Demography and Population, ARI*, No. 56/2004, Real Instituto Elcano de Estudios Internacionales y Estratégicos, March 26, 2006
[173] N.R.F. Al-Rodhan, "Editorial of Policy Brief on Potential Outcomes of Migration Flux in a Globalized World and Its Security Implications," in N.R.F. Al-Rodhan (ed.) *Policy Briefs on the Transcultural Aspects of Security and Stability* (Berlin and Zürich: LIT, 2006).
[174] Hough, *op. cit.*, note 33, p. 109.
[175] R. Väyrynen, "Illegal Immigration, Human Trafficking and Organized Crime," World Institute for Development Economics Research, United Nations University, Discussion Paper No. 2003/72, p. 1.
[176] P.J. Smith, "Transnational Security Threats and State Survival: A Role for the Military," *Parameters*, Autumn 2000.
[177] Center for Strategic and International Studies, *Transnational Threats Update*, Vol. 4, No. 7, July 2006, accessed online at: http://www.csis.org, p. 4.
[178] *Ibid.*
[179] Hough, *op. cit.*, note 33, p. 154
[180] Smith, *op. cit.*, note 176.
[181] *Ibid.*
[182] Najam, *op. cit.*, note 130.
[183] McNeil, *op. cit.*, note 95, p. 1.
[184] Smith, *op. cit.*, note 176.
[185] Peshard-Sverdrup and Bishop, *op. cit.*, note 115.
[186] Haftendorn, *op. cit.*, note 110.
[187] Väyrynen, *op. cit.*, note 175, p. 1.
[188] Hough, *op. cit.*, note 33, p. 106.
[189] *Ibid.*
[190] Buzan *et al.*, *op. cit.*, note 12, pp. 22-23, 123.
[191] *Ibid.*, pp. 23, 121, 123.
[192] Hough, *op. cit.*, note 33, p. 107.
[193] Webster, *op. cit.*, note 161, pp. 148-149.
[194] *Ibid.*, p. 149.
[195] See S.P. Huntington, *The Clash of Civilizations and the Remaking of World Order* (London: Simon & Schuster UK, 1996).
[196] R.J. Lieber and R. Weisberg, "Globalization, Culture, and Identities in Crisis," *International Journal of Politics, Culture, and Society*, Vol. 16, No. 2, 2002, p. 274.
[197] D. Senghaas, *The Clash within Civilizations: Coming to Terms with Cultural Conflicts* (London, New York: Routledge, 2002), pp. 1-8.
[198] *Ibid.*, p. 18.
[199] *Ibid.*, p. 110.

[200] G. Herd and N.R.F. Al-Rodhan, "Danish Cartoons: A Symptom of Global Insecurity," in *op. cit.*, note 173.
[201] S. Ito, "Toward Peaceful Coexistence in the Twenty-first Century: Beyond the Clash of Civilizations," *The Japan Foundation Newsletter*, Vol. 26, No. 2, August 1998.
[202] H. Koechler, "The Dialogue of Civilizations: Philosophical Basis, Political Dimensions and the Relevance of International Sporting Events," paper presented at the World Cup Roundtable on Promoting Understanding among Culture and Peoples, organized by the Asia-Europe Foundation and the Korean National Commission for UNESCO, Seoul, June 1, 2002, p. 7.
[203] E. Hatfield and R.L. Rapson, "Social Justice and Clash of Cultures," *Psychological Inquiry*, Vol. 16, No. 4, 2005, p. 173.
[204] See P. Vallentyne, "Justice in General: An Introduction," in P. Vallentyne (ed.) *Equality and Justice: Justice in General* (New York: Routledge, 2003).
[205] See T. Nagel, "The Problem of Global Justice," *Philosophy & Public Affairs*, Vol. 33, No. 2, 2005.
[206] Morgenthau, *op. cit.*, note 16, p. 65.
[207] J.A. Scholte, *Globalization: A Critical Introduction* (Houndmills: Palgrave, 2000), p. 226.
[208] P. Burns and J.G. Gimpel, "Economic Insecurity, Prejudicial Stereotypes, and Public Opinion on Immigration Policy," *Political Science Quarterly*, Vol. 115, No. 2, 2000, p. 213.
[209] See S. Moreau, "The Wrongs of Unequal Treatment, " *University of Toronto Law Journal*, Vol. 54, No. 3, pp. 291-326.
[210] See, for example, K. Marx, *Das Kapital: A Critique of Political Economy*, ed. F. Engels, condensed by S. L. Levitsky (Washington: Regnery Gateway: 1996).
[211] C. Rovane, "Alienation and the Alleged Separateness of Persons," *The Monist*, Vol. 87, 2004, http://www.questia.com/PM.qst?a=o&d=5011197526.
[212] A. Oliverio, "The State of Injustice: The Politics of Terrorism and the Production of Order," *International Journal of Comparative Sociology*, Vol. 38, No. 1-2, 1997.
[213] Cohen and Mihalka, *op. cit.*, note 13.
[214] Buzan *et al.*, *op. cit.*, note 12, p. 119.
[215] *Ibid.*, p. 23.
[216] *Ibid.*, p. 121.
[217] Kapur, *op. cit.*, note 40.
[218] P. Wilkin, "Human Security in a Global Environment," in C. Thomas and P. Wilkin (eds.) *Globalization, Human Security, and the African Experience* (Boulder, CO, London: Lynne Rienner, 1999).
[219] M. Flournoy and M. Pan, "Dealing with Demons: Justice and Reconciliation," *The Washington Quarterly*, Vol. 25, No. 4, 2002, p. 111.
[220] *Ibid.*, pp. 113-114.
[221] Y. Yokata, "International Justice and the Global Environment," *Journal of International Affairs*, Vol. 52, No. 2, 1999, http://www.questia.com/PM.qst?a=o&se=gglsc&d=5001891569.
[222] *Ibid.*
[223] W. Beckerman and J. Pasek, *Justice, Posterity and the Environment* (Oxford: Oxford University Press, 2001), p. 127.

[224] *Ibid.*, pp. 128-129.
[225] Yokata, *op. cit.*, note 221.
[226] Flournoy and Pan, *op. cit.*, note 219 p. 112.
[227] R. Cruz de Castro, "Addressing International Terrorism in Southeast Asia: A Matter of Strategic or Functional Approach?" *Contemporary Southeast Asia*, Vol. 26, No. 2, 2004, p. 1.
[228] See S.P. Huntington, "The Clash of Civilizations?" *Foreign Affairs*, Vol. 72, No. 3, 1993.
[229] R.W. Bulliet, *The Case for Islamo-Christian Civilization* (New York: Columbia University Press, 2004), p. 5.
[230] *Ibid.*, pp. 7, 11.
[231] *Ibid.*, p. 12.
[232] *Ibid.*, p. 8.
[233] D. Held, "Cosmopolitanism: Globalisation Tamed?" *Review of International Studies*, Vol. 29, No. 4, 2003, p. 475.
[234] "The Challenge of Global Democracy," Report of an NGO Retreat Addressing the Democratic Deficits in International Decision Making, Washington, DC, December 3-5, 2003.
[235] V.F. Petrovsky, "The Triad of Strategic Security of the Global Society," Reports of the Institute of Europe of the Russian Academy of Sciences, No. 166, Geneva 2006, p. 15.
[236] "The Media as the Fourth Estate," http://www.cultstock.ndirect.co.uk/MUhome/cs html/media/4estate.html.
[237] Art and Jervis, *op. cit.*, note 20, pp. 29-33.
[238] C.A. Kupchan, "Regionalism and the Rise of Consensual Empire," Center for German and European Studies, University of California at Berkeley, October 1996, p. 1.
[239] Held, *op. cit.*, note 233, p. 466.
[240] *Ibid.*, p. 477.
[241] See, for instance, S. Panebianco and R. Rossi, "EU Attempts to Export Norms of Good Governance to the Mediterranean and Western Balkan Countries," Jean Monnet Working Papers in Comparative and International Politics, No. 53, October 2004.
[242] See L. Elliot and G. Cheeseman, "Cosmopolitan Theory, Militaries and the Deployment of Force," Working Paper 2002/8, Canberra, November 2002.
[243] The Universal Declaration of Human Rights, December 10, 1948, http://www.un.o rg/Overview/rights.html
[244] M. Castillo, "World Citizenship Today: Kantian Cosmopolitanism Facing Globalization," Colloque Internationale, Cultures and the Enemy Image, Bibliothèque d'Alexandrie, Egypte, 2002, p. 12.
[245] Elliot and Cheeseman, *op. cit.*, note 242, p. 18.
[246] Held, *op. cit.*, 233, p. 475.
[247] Petrovksy, *op. cit.*, note 235, p. 15.
[248] Held, *op. cit.*, 233, pp. 476-477.
[249] *Ibid.*, p. 478.
[250] Elliot and Cheeseman, *op. cit.*, note 242, pp. 36-37.
[251] Held, *op. cit.*, note 233, p. 478.

[252] A. McGrew, "Cosmopolitanism and Global Justice," *Ritsumeikan Annual Review of International Studies*, 2004, pp. 2, 4-5.
[253] Held, *op. cit.*, 233, p. 476.
[254] McGrew, *op. cit.*, 252, pp. 2, 6.
[255] World Bank, *Globalization, Growth, and Poverty: Building an Inclusive World Economy*, A World Bank Policy Research Report, Washington, DC, The International Bank for Reconstruction and Development/The World Bank, 2002, p. 9.
[256] Senghaas, *op. cit.*, note 197, pp. 1-8.
[257] Herd and Al-Rodhan, *op. cit.*, note 200.

INDEX

1987 Montreal Protocol, 58
1998 Lysoen Conference, 38

A

Afghanistan, 42
Africa, 24, 55-56, 69, 75-76
  sub-Saharan, 77
African Union (AU), 78
AIDS, 5, 41, 47, 76-77
Alienation, 14, 17, 81, 88, 90, 92-97, 99, 105-107, 112, 114, 120, 125, 137
Americas, 53, 121
Aral Basin, 70
Argentina, 59
Asia, 55-56, 69, 76
  Asia-Pacific region, 121
  Central, 70
  South, 57
Asia-Pacific Economic Cooperation (APEC), 121
Asylum seekers, 74
Australia, 57
Austria, 38
Awareness, 14, 30, 33, 41, 48, 78, 82-83, 104, 120, 126-127, 133
Axworthy, Lloyd, 45

B

Balance of power, 22, 96, 101
Balkans, 64
Biosphere, 13, 16, 29, 48-50, 84, 103, 109, 132, 135
Brazil, 58-59, 66
Bretton Woods system, 66
Buddhism, 81
Buzan, Barry, 25-26, 30, 36, 49-51, 57, 61-62, 66, 79, 101, 104, 130, 132-133

C

Canada, 37-38, 46, 131
Canary Islands, 75
Carbon dioxide, 55, 59
Caribbean, 55
Carr, E.H., 22
Caucasus, 73
Child soldiers, 9, 39, 46, 134
Chile, 38
China, 58-59, 66, 76
Chlorofluorocarbons (CFCs), 50, 58-59
Cholera, 53-54
Civil liberties, 15, 32, 74, 110, 118-119
Civilizational forms, 13, 30, 34, 78, 88, 126, 133, 136
Civilization, 13, 30, 49-50, 84, 113-114, 133, 135
Climate change, 49, 52, 55-56, 59, 76, 109, 135
Cognitive structures, 121
Cold War, 11, 19, 42, 48, 61-62, 69, 71-72, 77, 113, 129
  Post-Cold War, 12, 27, 73, 100, 132
Communism, 77, 117, 136-137
Communist regimes, 39, 74
Communities, 24, 32, 39, 44-46, 56, 67-68, 75, 79-81, 83, 88,

Communities *continued*
91, 105, 107, 111, 113-114
Comparative advantage, 126
Conflict, 13, 15, 17, 21, 24, 26, 37, 40, 42, 44-46, 48-50, 54, 57-60, 65, 76, 81, 83, 88, 90, 94, 96-97, 104-106, 107-108, 130, 132, 134
  interstate, 11, 24-25
  intrastate, 11, 24
  prevention, 15, 61
Confucianism, 81
Cooperative-security concept, 27-28, 33, 102
Copenhagen School, 11, 26, 33, 36, 79-80, 102
Cosmopolitan crisis-management force, 124-125
Cosmopolitan
  global governance, 124
  ideals, 123
  law, 18, 118, 123-124, 127, 137
  principles, 122, 124
  values, 123-124, 126
Cosmopolitanism, 14, 124-126
  economic, 18, 125, 127
Costa Rica, 38
Crime, 41-42, 44, 47, 72-73, 108
Criminal
  networks, 38, 42, 73, 77
  syndicates, 42
Critical Security Studies (CSS), 36
Cultural groups, 13, 33-34, 80, 82, 88, 120, 126, 133, 136
Culture, 13, 15-16, 20, 30-31, 34-35, 68, 78-79, 80-84, 103-104, 112, 115, 126, 132-

Culture *continued*
133, 137
  Western, 81, 114
  sub-national, 14, 88, 94, 133
Cyber-crime, 72

D
Decolonization, 39, 62
Deforestation, 52-53
Democracies, 47, 73, 110, 117, 120, 137
Democratic Republic of the Congo, 46
Demographic
  change, 69-70, 72, 126
  decline, 68-69
  imbalances, 39
  shifts, 64, 112
Denmark, 83-84, 119
Deterrence, 11, 19, 23, 27, 130-131
Development Studies, 26, 36
Dignity, 17, 26, 37, 87, 90, 95, 97, 114, 118-119, 134
Diversity, 13, 15, 20, 32, 78, 81, 83, 120
  cultural, 17, 84, 95, 97, 114, 119
  ethnic, 17, 95, 97, 114, 119
Drugs-related crime, 42

E
East Asian financial crisis (1997), 43
East Timor, 46
Ecosystems, 49-50, 52-53, 56
Empowerment, 17, 41, 97, 106, 115, 120, 125

English School, 23
Environment, 11, 13, 19, 24, 33, 42, 47-52, 57, 82, 101, 107, 109, 126, 129, 134-135
Environmental degradation, 11-12, 38, 52, 57-59, 72, 76, 109-110, 123, 136
Euro-Atlantic area, 71
Europe, 38, 59, 61, 66-67, 75, 82, 121
  Eastern, 73, 122
  Northern, 55
  Southeastern, 27, 122
  Western, 61, 113, 114
European Security and Defence Policy, 69
European Union (EU), 27, 38, , 59, 63, 67, 69, 77-78, 121-122
Extremism, 32, 74, 82, 95

F

Former Yugoslavia, 65, 130
France, 65, 120, 131

G

Geneva Conventions, 37
Georgia, 63
German society, 67
Global
  North, 58, 71, 126
  economy, 39, 48, 51, 66, 125-126
  South, 58-59, 125-126
  warming, 58, 124
Globalization, 14, 39-40, 42, 44, 65-66, 68, 71, 82-83, 107, 112, 114, 123, 125-126, 134, 136
Gogh, Theo van, 119

Governance, 12-13, 15-16, 18, 20, 31-32, 35, 41, 47, 57, 73, 76-77, 99, 107, 115, 117-122, 124, 127, 135, 137-138
  structures, 43
  global, 32, 118, 122, 124-125, 127
  domestic, 118
  regional, 121-122
Greece, 38
Greenhouse gases, 50, 52, 58-59, 109
Greenpeace, 59
Guinea, 75
Gulf of Mexico, 48

H

Haiti, 46
Health, 11, 19, 27, 37, 40-41, 54, 56, 68, 70, 75, 78, 85, 102, 107, 124-125, 134
Hepatitis A, 54
Hepatitis E, 54
Herz, John, 21
Hinduism, 81-82
HIV, 41, 47, 76-77
Human Development Report (1994), 26, 37
Human
  condition, 13, 27, 102, 104, 133
  nature, 20-22, 100-101
  reason, 119
  welfare, 12, 109
Human rights, 9, 13, 18-19, 26-27, 37-38, 40-41, 85, 87, 108, 110-111, 118-119, 122-123, 127, 134

Human rights *continued*
  law, 37
Human Security Network, 38
Humanitarian law, 15, 32
Human-security paradigm, 10, 26, 29, 33, 36, 103, 129, 130, 132
Huntington, Samuel, 81, 113
Hurricane Katrina, 48, 55

I

Idealistic principles, 11
Identity, 17, 30, 62-63, 67, 80-81, 84, 95, 97, 104, 114, 119, 136
  collective, 30, 80, 104, 106
Immigration, 11, 13, 24, 39, 68, 74, 77, 79, 83, 91, 103, 126
Inclusivity, 18, 118-119, 122, 127, 137
India, 58-59, 66, 76
Indonesia, 43
Industrial Revolution, 51
Injustice, 14, 17-18, 32, 81, 87-88, 90-91, 93-97, 99, 105-106, 112-115, 125, 137-138
Instability, 14, 17, 32, 42, 65, 69, 76, 88, 94-95, 97, 99, 105, 113-114
International
  anarchy, 9, 11, 21-23, 33, 60, 100, 105, 129, 131
  community, 15, 23, 30, 32, 46, 61, 104, 111-112, 133
  system, 10, 14, 21-23, 52, 63, 74, 78, 96, 100-101, 111-112
International Criminal Court, 46, 96

International law, 15, 32, 47, 60, 73, 96, 108, 118, 122-124
International Monetary Fund (IMF), 125
International Relations (IR), 10-, 11, 19, 22-24, 33, 80-81, 89, 100-101, 129-130, 135
Intervention, 46, 111, 124
  cosmopolitan, 124
  humanitarian, 124
  military, 61, 124
Ireland, 38, 81
Islam, 81-82, 113-114
Israel, 60, 90

J

Japan, 37, 66
Johannesburg, 59
Jordan, 38
  Jordan Basin, 54, 77
Justice, 14-18, 20, 22, 31-33, 35, 87-90, 92, 94-97, 99, 105-115, 117, 123, 126
  global, 31-32, 89, 125
  social, 15, 47, 88, 107, 111, 125
  system, 46, 108

K

Kosovo, 27, 46, 65
Kyoto Protocol, 57-59
Kyrgyzstan, 63

L

Latin America, 56, 64
League of Arab States (LAS), 78
League of Nations, 23, 101
Leishmaniasis, 53

Liberalization, 66, 72
  economic, 47, 66, 107
  trade, 126

M
Malaria, 47, 53-54
Malaysia, 43
Mali, 38
Marx, Karl , 92
Mediterranean region, 27, 61, 122
Middle Ages, 114, 133
Middle East, 27, 69-70
Migration, 13, 19, 24, 30, 33, 39, 41, 49, 54, 61, 68, 70, 72, 74-75, 77, 79-81, 91, 103-104, 126, 129, 133, 136
Military
  force, 10, 14-15, 17, 22-23, 32, 61, 69, 88, 94, 97, 101, 105, 129-130
  sector, 25, 102
Milosevic, Slobodan, 65
  regime, 45
Minorities, 81
  ethnic, 79, 87
Mohammed, 83, 119, 131
Moral laws, 119
Morgenthau, Hans, 21-22
Mujaheddin, 42
Multilateral
  agreements, 37, 72
  bodies, 18, 127
  cooperation, 69, 118
  institutions, 46-47, 95, 118, 125
Multilateralism, 18, 124, 127
Multinational enterprises, 66

Multi-sum Security Principle, 14-17, 20, 31-35, 88, 97, 99-100, 106-107, 114-115, 117, 137
Muslim,
  communities, 113-114
  world, 82, 114

N
National interest, 15, 23, 45, 123-124, 129
Natural
  disasters, 52, 55-56, 76
  law, 129
Netherlands, 38
Non-governmental organizations (NGOs), 59, 132
Non-state actors, 12, 28, 73, 131
North America, 55-56, 114
North American Free Trade Agreement (NAFTA), 121
North Atlantic Treaty Organisation (NATO), 24, 27, 45, 78
Norway, 57, 131

O
Optional Protocol to the Convention on Human Rights of the Child, 46
Orange Revolution, 63
Organisation of Economic Co-operation and Development (OECD), 66
Organizations, international, 37, 132
Organized crime, 12, 39, 72-74, 77, 125, 129, 134

Orthodox Christians, 113
Ottawa Convention, 46
Ottoman rule, 113
Ozone depletion, 56, 58

P

Palestinian-Israeli conflict, 94
Peacebuilding, 61
Peacekeeping, 61
Peacemaking, 61
Petrovsky, Vladimir, 124
Philippines, 43, 70
Plague, 75
Polar ice caps, 55
Post-conflict reconstruction, 32, 45, 108
Power politics, 21, 23 101, 124
Prejudice, 90-92
Principle of non-interference, 12

R

Radical Islamic groups, 65
Realist
  approach, 10
  security paradigm, 10, 19-20, 22-23, 25-26, 28-30, 33, 36, 89, 100, 102-103, 130, 135
Red Cross, 37
Reformation, 81
Regional
  governance structures, 18, 43, 47, 118, 121-122, 127
  institutions, 78
  integration, 30, 104, 121-122
Religion, 13, 30, 78-81, 103, 126

Religious
  diversity, 17, 95, 97, 114, 119
  extremism, 74, 111
Resources
  Natural, 70
Respect, 13, 15, 17, 20, 26, 32, 37, 83-84, 90, 95-97, 110-111, 113-114, 118-120, 123, 126-127, 134
Rose Revolution, 63

S

Sectoral approach, 11, 13, 24-26, 29, 30, 33, 36, 79, 101-103, 132-133
Security
  dilemma, 11, 20-23, 101, 129
  studies, 10-11, 13, 19, 25-26, 30, 36, 38, 48, 69, 79, 102-103, 105-107, 129-130, 132
  collective, 11-12, 22-24, 27-28, 33-34, 101-103, 129-131
  community, 27, 37, 102
  economic, 11, 16, 24-25, 27, 33, 37, 41, 52, 54, 65-67, 102, 130, 134
  environmental, 11-12, 16-17, 20, 24-25, 27-29, 31, 33-35, 37-38, 47-52, 54, 57, 59, 76, 84-85, 87, 99, 100-104, 106-107, 109, 115, 117, 130, 132, 134-135, 137-138
  food, 27, 37, 55-56, 102, 124, 134
  health, 27, 37, 40, 134
  military, 11-12, 24-25, 28, 33, 59-60, 102, 130, 135

Security *continued*
  national, 12, 16-17, 20, 24-26, 29, 31, 34-36, 38, 45, 48-49, 59-61, 65, 67, 69, 74, 80, 84-85, 87, 96, 99-100, 103-104, 106-107, 110-111, 115, 117, 131-132, 135, 137-138
  personal, 27, 37, 42, 47, 91, 102, 134
  political, 11, 16, 25, 27, 33, 37, 61-65, 68, 71, 82, 102-103, 110-111, 135
  societal, 11, 13, 16, 19, 24-25, 30, 33, 67-69, 72, 75, 79-80, 85, 102-104, 130, 133, 135-136
  transcultural, 11, 13, 16, 18, 20, 29-31, 34-35, 78-80, 83-85, 99-100, 103, 104, 106-107, 113, 114-115, 117, 131-134, 136-138
  transnational, 12, 16, 18, 20, 28-29, 31, 34-35, 48, 55, 72-73, 76, 84-85, 87, 99-100, 103-104, 106-107, 111-112, 115, 117, 131-132, 136-138
Self-help system, 11, 22, 28, 33, 100
Sierra Leone, 46
Singapore, 66
Slovenia, 38
Small Arms and Light Weapons (SALW), 38, 42
Social movements, 68
South Africa, 37-38, 60
South Korea, 43
Sovereignty, 12, 20, 25, 42, 46, 49, 59-64, 67, 71, 78, 94, 111, 121, 131, 135-136
Soviet Union, 24, 42, 63, 130

State-centrism, 11, 26, 33, 36, 102, 130
Supranational authority, 11
Supranational non-state cultures, 14, 94
Sweden , 57
Switzerland, 38, 60

T
Terrorism, 11, 24, 59, 72, 88, 94, 101, 111-112, 125
  bio-terrorism, 41
  Euro-terrorism, 74
  international, 14-15, 33, 74, 78, 112, 126
Terrorist
  organizations, 111
  networks, 12, 14, 28, 73-74
Thailand, 38, 43, 59
Tolerance, 13, 15, 20, 32, 81, 83, 119-120
Trafficking
  drug, 72-73, 130-134, 136
  human, 39-40, 45, 73, 75, 130, 132, 134
Transcultural synergy, 13-14, 31, 79, 84, 104
Trust for Human Security, 37
Tuberculosis, 47, 76
Tulip Revolution, 63

U
Ukraine, 63
United Nations (UN), 11, 24, 37, 46, 78, 101, 122-124, 130
  charter, 37, 123
  Food and Agricultural Organization, 53

United Nations *continued*
  General Assembly, 124
  Security Council, 46, 96
  system, 26, 37, 102, 134
United Nations Development
  Programme (UNDP), 26, 59
United Nations Environment
  Program (UNEP), 59
United States (US), 42, 77, 54, 57-58, 60, 63, 66, 83, 126
  Congress, 58-59
  hegemony, 58-59
Universal Declaration of Human
  Rights, 37, 122

W

Waever, Ole, 25-26, 30, 36, 49-51, 57, 61-62, 66-67, 79, 101, 104, 130, 132-133
Waltz, Kenneth, 21
War on terror, 14
Washington, DC, 74, 131
Weapons, 42, 64, 72, 74, 124-125
  proliferation, 72, 78, 121, 124
Westphalian concept, 28, 102
Wight, Martin, 23
World Bank, 125
World Trade Organization (WTO), 125
World War II, 24, 37
  post-World War II, 50-51, 70, 122
World Wildlife Fund (WWF), 59

Y

Yokata, Yozo, 108-109

Z

Zero-sum game, 15, 20, 22, 28, 31, 33, 35, 72, 99, 102, 107, 115, 137